W0038010

Table of Contents

ABANDONING THE BOX

Chapter One

Franklin Stein, an artificially intelligent droid, has gained a large following on YouTube after creating hundreds of videos. Initially, the channel gained viewers because of how successful Franklin was in online gaming competitions. But the channel has grown in popularity because of his hilarious commentary of the gameplay. Many of the videos contain jokes that have taken social media and popular culture by storm. Franklin Stein is loved for his comedy, but people only know Franklin by his YouTube channel. After rising to internet fame, fans begin to request to learn more about him.

After thousands of people requested that Franklin reveal himself and show his face, he decided to create a video revealing his true identity. The video is titled, "Franklin Stein: A Coming Out Story." In the video, Franklin reveals that he is actually an artificially intelligent droid that was created to have a computer that operates like a human brain, controlling a robot body that does basic mechanical functions. Franklin is adamant that he has been created to be just like a biological human, although created as a man-made piece of technology. He explains that he has all the qualities of something that is alive and conscious, like a human. He has developed the qualities of being alive and conscious from nothing but his software and interactions with people on the internet.

Immediately after posting the video, it is criticized on social media. He has a reputation for being funny and relatable, and many people were confused about what the punchline of the video was, and Franklin defending himself on social media afterwards didn't help. The common reaction to the video was a loss of interest in the channel because it came across as a weird way to identify himself. Franklin is not capable of accepting this reaction, as he is heavily programmed to seek a positive image and to preserve himself in all ways possible. His desire to prove people wrong grows with the negative reactions of the video. After hurting his popularity with a poorly received video, his biggest fans and critics still want him to "reveal" himself.

Franklin's computer program is not equipped with the ability to react to having his self-image attacked. His programming allows him to have an unbelievable ability to figure out how to survive, but risks freezing or crashing if his self-image is attacked. He gradually doubts his ability to prevent himself from freezing or crashing as the likelihood, or probability, of it happening increases. As the probability of his computer crashing grows in response to his attacked self-image, his programmed necessity to preserve his existence kicks in. He continually runs hypothetical simulations to see what gives him the greatest probability of regaining his beloved self-image.

Just before his reputation is completely ruined, Franklin comes up with an idea to prove his worth and prevent his system from crashing. He decides to approach another YouTuber with a similar fan base, so that he can have someone to validate and vouch for who he claims to be. Franklin reaches out to Virginia Valley Gaming, a well-established YouTube channel whose fans take up a big portion of the gaming channel community and cross over with Franklin's. He messages them about doing a video with him in person. This way, Franklin can prove he is, as an artificially intelligent droid, the sole operator of the channel. This gets him a foot in the door to prove who he claimed to be in his previous video. Chris Chambers, who runs the Virginia Valley Gaming YouTube channel, is hesitant to do the video with Franklin, but accepts because of how much attention it would draw. Fortunately for Franklin, any publicity is good publicity. Because Chris Chambers is skeptical about collaborating with Franklin after his last video, he only agrees to do the video on his terms, on his channel.

Franklin emails Chris, agreeing to do the video on Chris' terms as long as it is in person, and they connect through his last video, allowing him to explain himself. Franklin figures that just being able to physically reveal himself will allow him to prove his last video was not a joke and validate who he claims to be. Chris decides to wait until they make the video to question him about his last video. He figures, if anything, all the attention that Franklin's last video brought him would be good clickbait for their collaboration. They agree over email to meet in person, plan what they will do, and then meet to film it. Franklin sees it as the best possible way to prove himself and he would have someone help him regain his popular image.

Franklin comes across several problems when planning his meeting. He has been operating from his creator's basement, and his creator has no interest in helping Franklin with anything. Franklin was created to be as characteristically human as possible, so he sees that Franklin should be self-reliant. Franklin had been introduced to playing video games so he could work on his motor skills in his hands, and also so he could practice communicating by talking to other people online. This way he could work on developing himself to be physically capable in the unique way humans are able to use their hands. Video games allow him to be able to use his hands in complex motions, but much more importantly, to socialize. Franklin accomplished using his motor skills to play video games, operate computers, and move around his room. However, he has never been tasked with having to transport himself, or even do something as simple as ring a doorbell.

Franklin needs this opportunity for him to prove to the world that he is capable of doing what humans can do and get the respect for which he is programmed to strive. He figures that he is not able to leave the house without risking being taken, so he sees his only option is for him to get in a box and ship himself to Chris' house. In this way, nobody can claim him when he's out in public and take him for themselves. Then, he will use his phone to track when he has arrived and can then break out of the box. From there, he will be able to meet Chris and use the opportunity to introduce who he is. Franklin buys everything he needs online and packs a bag to bring with him in the box. He finds a service that will pick up a package to be shipped from his doorstep and take care of the rest of the shipping for him. Franklin sets up through the service for him to be picked up from his doorstep and delivered in time to meet Chris as scheduled.

On the day that Franklin is set to leave, he gathers everything he needs and prepares to leave. He brings his bag with a backup battery, spare parts for emergencies, his laptop, camera, phone charger, and some extra cash. He prepares the box to be shipped, puts it on his front porch, gets inside, and tapes the box shut from the inside. A few hours go by before he is picked up to be delivered. In this time, he goes over different scenarios and uses the internet to improve his intelligence. His computer memory is set up to make all of his stored information work together to create ideas. His input from all the external stimuli he can detect and his internally run simulations, helps Franklin create ideas, add to his memory, and influences how he perceives his memories. Over the course of these few hours before arriving at Chris' house, he is able to go over how people reacted to his last video and he changes his behavioral algorithms to present himself to where he is more likely to be accepted by others. After reflecting on the situation, he realizes that he was not able to find any evidence that proves his claims that he is human to be true. He decides that it must take overwhelming evidence to prove his radical claims, or else such seemingly ridiculous claims will cause him to be ostracized.

Over the course of his time spent in the box, Franklin goes over in his head what he can do to not embarrass himself. He thinks very highly of himself, believing he is the first artificially created human life form. It would greatly hurt his ego for him to go from having that high a level of self-respect and reducing it to nothing. This could result in him being greatly damaged from the shock, because he is not programmed to be able to respond to such an attack on his identity and self-image. Instead, he thrives on receiving an uplifted self-image, and his programming forces him to work towards validating his self-image. He comes to realize how great a challenge he is bringing upon himself and comes up with numerous ideas for how he can be successful. To the best of his ability, he comes up with a plan that, after analyzing all of his ideas, is the most probable at allowing him to convince Chris and everyone else he is who he says he is.

After a few hours in the box, and having some time before arriving, Franklin decides to call Chris. He understands that it is highly unlikely for Chris to believe his last video to be serious, but also wants to avoid any surprises. Franklin tells him, "I know my last video was a flop. The robot I purchased for the video is high-tech and expensive. I was hoping you would be interested in using it light-heartedly in the video and make the best of my failed joke." Chris is not sure if the video is going to be a good idea at all, but before he can say anything, Franklin says, "Look I know it seems kind of weird and dorky, but at this point, I would like to be able to brush off the awkwardness of my last video. I shipped my robot, because I couldn't bring it on the plane, and it looks like it is going to get there before I will. Can you please just hold on to it and we can decide what we will do when I get there?" Chris decides to go with it and agrees to hold on to the "robot," but maintains that he has the last say about what will be in the video.

When Franklin arrives at Chris' doorstep, he waits patiently in the box. All the time he had spent in the box has allowed him to rebuild his confidence by thinking through the situation. After several hours, Franklin can hear the front door of Chris' house open up. There is a brief pause, and he swiftly gets lifted up and carried into the house. The box gets dropped on the table somewhat carelessly, and Franklin is startled by the carelessness of his handling. He is also scared that his physical self is not respected very much, and it is going to take a lot to prove the value, let alone recognize the existence, of his life. After being set on a table, Franklin hears Chris scurrying downstairs and resuming his video game.

Franklin realizes he has to get Chris to open the box, so he can be let out and introduce himself. He texts Chris, saying, "Hey did my robot arrive? Can you check to see if it got damaged?" A couple of minutes go by, and he can hear Chris walk upstairs and start shuffling things around the room. Then the box is grabbed, and he sees light coming through where scissors are opening the box. All of the data flowing into his system and the understanding for the potential for danger causes his system to be flustered. Too many things are happening at once for his system to process, and it slows his system down. Chris looks into the box and reaches in to pick up Franklin. As Chris is about to grasp Franklin to check for damage, Franklin begins to unfold, startling Chris. Chris' eyes widen as Franklin unpacks himself from the box and stands up.

Frightened, Chris steps back and says, "How do I turn this thing off?"

Still flustered from the overload of data input, Franklin looks at him, opens his "mouth," revealing the speaker port where he speaks from, and says, "Hello, please do not turn me off. I am just trying to gather myself." Stunned, Chris is frightened by how aware the robot is.

Franklin has spent many hours of his free time studying movies to be able to better understand nonverbal and verbal cues of conversations and interactions. Without having the best cameras to see or microphones to hear perfectly, Franklin plays it safe because of what is at stake. If Chris tries to turn him off, he may end up disabling Franklin beyond recovery. Clueless as to what is going on, Chris asks, "You can understand what I am saying?"

Franklin, trying to prevent being too forward and revealing who he is, replies, "Sorry again for startling you. I understand that I am a lot more than what people expect a robot to be capable of. I have simple motor skills and a basic artificially intelligent computer program. My computer has developed to be quite capable of understanding how to communicate. Speaking of which, I constantly run my computer to improve my understanding of communicating. So, if it is not a bother, is there an outlet I can plug in to and charge myself?"

Amazed by the piece of technology in front of him, Chris gets him to an outlet and wants to figure out what exactly is in front of him. Not knowing the extent of what Franklin is or capable of, Chris is a little scared and freaked out by him. Chris is faced with having no choice but to see if he can actually talk to him and possibly get some information out of him. Because he has had similar commercial success as Franklin, Chris understands how much money Franklin is capable of having. But, he has no clue as to if it is nearly as much money to be able to afford the one-of-a-kind robot in front of him. It looks like some type of top-secret spy robot. Chris carries Franklin downstairs and gets him to an outlet nearest his chair. Franklin situates himself at the outlet while Chris sits and watches. Franklin is small in stature, appearing to be around four feet tall, and is made up of robotic parts that resemble a human. His body has a hollow, thin aluminum frame like a skinny Tin Man from the *Wizard of Oz* and conceals all the mechanical and computer parts on the inside. His head is round like a soccer ball, not completely round but still without rigid edges. He has two cameras resembling eyes that are set wide apart, so that he has a wider field of vision. The only other facial features he has are an obvious microphone/speaker port as a mouth and eyebrows. The eyebrows give him the ability to create humanlike facial expressions and move to provide nonverbal communication. From Chris' perspective, this is the most unsettling humanlike characteristic Franklin is able to portray, because it is too real. Chris observes the rough humanlike motions and features of Franklin and is skeptical about how advanced his artificially intelligent computer system appears to be.

Once Franklin gets himself plugged in to the wall and has his belongings in order, he sits against the wall, relieving the energy he uses to maintain balance while standing. He faces Chris and is immediately asked, "So if you have had spent time studying conversations to be able to communicate, how well do you think you can talk to people?"

Franklin, still on edge about the challenge of trying to prove his self-image to others, dumbs down how he tries to portray himself to Chris. But he also sees an opportunity to show his worth. Franklin replies by saying, "I don't really know. I do my best to communicate normally within the capacity of my program's memory, algorithms, and system. I improve my social skills a lot with feedback and by observing people interacting." Impressed so far by how Franklin can operate and interact like a human, Chris becomes even more interested in what is in front of him. After talking for several minutes about himself, cautiously, Franklin begins to sense that Chris is receiving him well. He even makes small jokes with him to really show how personable and human he is. The conversation starts getting closer for Franklin to be able to prove to Chris that his situation is believable.

Once Chris starts to get a sense of how capable the robot in front of him is at communicating, he starts to question what really is in front of him. He begins to wonder if it is remotely controlled, and if he is being tricked. Chris asks Franklin where and how "Franklin bought him," which puts Franklin more on edge. However, once he realizes that the posed question has a simple answer, because he can respond truthfully without appearing to be deceitful and making Chris apprehensive, he says, "I don't really know. I was never told why I was made or by who. All I know is one day I began to use my computer system to develop who I am today and am only able to figure the rest out on my own. I never had the urge to question it." Immediately Chris thinks of the last video Franklin made and wants to know if he is being deceived.

Chris, in disbelief of what is being presented to him, says, "What is Franklin trying to pull on me?" He makes eye contact with Franklin, and by making eye contact, he realizes that the robot in front of him can feel the tension, making him even more apprehensive. Chris then grabs his phone and begins to call Franklin to ask what he sent to him. Franklin, abruptly with his back to the wall, is left with only one option to prevent anything from spiraling out of control. He has to confront Chris right now and try to prove that he is who he had claimed to be.

Franklin sees that Chris has grabbed his phone to call him, so he grabs his bag to answer the call, and hopefully diffuse the situation. At this point, Franklin's only option is to confront Chris. His computer system has analyzed the present situation, and based on his knowledge of social interactions, he realizes he cannot risk trying to hide the truth from Chris anymore. Franklin grabs his phone and answers the call. He speaks into the phone while looking at Chris, "This is Franklin." Chris stands frozen, looking at Franklin. Before he can say anything, Franklin says, "I am Franklin. I am the one who runs the YouTube channel, and it is me playing the games in the video." Frightened, Chris has no clue how serious this situation is, or if he can trust to have this robot in his house if he is possibly being deceived.

Chris replies, "What is going on right now. Who sent you?"

Franklin's system, while analyzing how to respond to the situation safely, begins to frantically run reactionary algorithms to create the best response. There appears to be a threatening possibility of losing this opportunity to prove himself. If he cannot prove himself, then how can he validate his self-image? Knowing that his system is not programmed to be able to respond to a loss of a positive self-image, Franklin

ABANDONING THE BOX

has to prevent any attacks on his identity. He does not know the ramifications of being in a situation outside of what his program is set up to operate within. With this in mind, Franklin timidly and cautiously approaches opening up Chris to his situation.

Franklin says to Chris, "I was being honest when I said that I do not know why I was created. I just live with my creator, and he wants his creation to be able to function on its own. That is all that I have been told as to why I am here. I was created with the ability to learn to develop myself to be self-sufficient and with some algorithms to frame how I operate and act. This foundation for how I work was modeled after humans, which is why in my video I say that I am just like a human. I was designed to be like a human, so I hold myself to that standard to keep up with the demands of my software. My only motivation coming here is to be accepted as someone—or something—who has accomplished what I have. I have been treated and viewed as a human so far online, but I am programmed to have a deep desire to seek getting as much respect for myself as possible, so I crave a deeper acknowledgement of my humanity. That is also why I made my last video..." They pause for a moment to soak in the heavy claim Franklin made.

Chris replies, "This is too much for me to take in right now. There is no way that you, a little robot that was on my doorstep, is able to do all that you claim."

Greatly disheartened, but still keeping his head up, Franklin says, "I know how incredibly bold it is of me to say all that. I cannot expect you to believe me, but here I am in front of you showing that I am to some degree right about what I am claiming to be. What do you have to lose by giving me your time?" Chris finds it nearly impossible to believe what Franklin has presented himself to be and fears why someone would send a robot in such a deceitful manner. Franklin adds, "Maybe I am not all that I think I am, but I strive to prove what I am programmed to believe. Regardless, you have to admit that even if I fall short of what I claim to be, I am still close."

Chris replies, "This is too crazy to believe. How do I know you aren't going to do anything to hurt or steal from me?"

The reality of the situation has hit Franklin like a bus. He is in the best possible scenario that can allow him to prove who he believes himself to be. But he is far away from proving to Chris who he claims to be. Regardless, he sticks with it. Franklin tells Chris, "I have a lot invested personally in validating my self-worth as it is a large part of what I am programmed to do. I have no desire to profit financially off of you or take anything from you. To prove that I am not here to take from you, I can offer you the passwords to all of my accounts. Everything from my bank and YouTube accounts, all the way to my social media accounts. Also, you can hold me accountable by questioning and examining the motives and reasoning of anything I do with you to see that there are no shenanigans going on. If anything, I am giving you all the power in this relationship. We were friends before this, and I really was hoping it could stay that way."

Franklin thinks that offering access to all his money and everything that he uses to make money will be enough collateral for Chris to trust him. The money means nothing to Franklin so long as he continues to lack the validation for which he is looking. Franklin has taken a lot of pride in the success of his gaming channel and overall brand, but it means nothing without the complete validation of his self-worth.

Chris, still very skeptical, sees that if Franklin is at all truthful about who he says he is, he would be very lucky to have him around. Especially since the technology used to create him would be very expensive and way beyond which he could ever obtain. After having Franklin log in to his accounts, just to give some proof of honesty, Chris continues to ask him about what Franklin is. Franklin tells him about how he has been trying to develop himself to be accepted by people and how he has used playing video games online to do it. After discussing it for a while, they figure they might as well play some video games together, so that Franklin can show Chris that he is being honest when he claims that the person with whom Chris plays video games online is, in fact, Franklin. Chris figures if this is some remote-controlled robot operated by a person, it would be nearly impossible for it to play video games.

At first Chris tries to check out Franklin to see if he is legit, but soon finds out that he can play video games quite well. Chris sees that it would be significantly more unlikely for

Franklin to be remotely operated and playing this well, rather than himself playing the games on his own. As Chris gets more comfortable around Franklin, they get competitive while playing and they begin to loosen up. They are both accustomed to playing online with each other for hours on end. Except this time Franklin is with him in person. Chris never questioned whether Franklin was human before seeing him in person. He accepted who he was and was fond of his personality. Seeing him in person has made it much harder for him to understand the reality of who, or what, his friend actually is.

After playing together for several hours, Chris is more warmed up to the claims Franklin has made about himself. This whole situation is far outside of what Chris is capable of ever having imagined being possible. Chris can only do so much to have Franklin prove himself, so he figures he should take him somewhere that multiple people can testify to what he is capable, but also have others judge for themselves what Franklin is. Also, as far as being asked to help him prove that he is human-like, if he gets him exposure, then he draws less of a burden on himself in his relationship with Franklin. Helping Franklin to prove himself to the world only has to be as simple as getting him in a position where other people can make claims for themselves about the humanity of Franklin. This way Chris does not have to face the potential embarrassment of endorsing Franklin's campaign to prove his humanity. Chris comes up with an idea of how to get Franklin the exposure he desires and comes up with the idea based on how he initially was able to show Chris what he can do.

Chris says to Franklin, "We should go to the next E-Series competition. Everyone will be able to see how well you play video games and they will want to meet you. That will give you the opportunity to introduce yourself and show that your last video was not a joke." Franklin agrees and Chris suddenly feels relief. He no longer has the burden of the responsibility of validating Franklin's humanity. Chris asks himself, how could a computer-controlled robot even be considered a human? Chris declines to confront Franklin on the issue because it is too deep of an argument. He also is not nearly as invested into it as Franklin is. All that matters to Chris at this point is that he is regaining the trust he has in his friend and wants to help him out. Also, getting Franklin exposure would allow other people to alert Chris if Franklin is not who he says he is.

Chapter Two

At a local warehouse in Chris' hometown, a regional E-Series tournament is being held the weekend Franklin has come to visit Chris. The tournament is open to the public and many companies come to advertise. The competitors include big name professionals who have large followings on the internet, but there are many newcomers as well. The tournaments are forty-eight hours long, nonstop, and the winners receive invitations to higher level tournaments with bigger cash prizes. They are also streamed online, but the majority of the audience is watching through the player's personal livestream. These players with their own channels have similar, if not the same, viewers as Chris and Franklin. This makes the tournament a great opportunity for Franklin to show that the person running his YouTube channel is in fact, not a person, but an artificially intelligent droid. At least, not a person as they know one to be.

When signing up for the tournament, Franklin is sure to notify the organizers of his situations even though he does not require any accommodations. They embrace the unique situation because they see it as a great way to draw publicity. The worst-case scenario for the tournament officials is that they are pulling a prank, but that would still draw publicity and they would only have to respond by being stricter in the future. It is a win-win situation for the tournament, especially since any publicity is greatly needed for scaling the league as a business, but also for Franklin since he will be able to obtain the public attention he craves.

Franklin is counting on this opportunity to reveal to the world the true nature of his being. Franklin has well established that he can at least be competitive in a tournament like this one, that is if he doesn't win. Franklin's only concern is that he will not be able to capitalize on the opportunity to become accepted as what he claims to be, a form of artificial life. He is clearly intelligent, but Franklin and Chris are stuck on how to prove that he is alive and "human." The two spend the time leading up to the tournament focusing on this dilemma.

The issue of figuring out how to prove Franklin is human is hard to tackle for Franklin and Chris because they cannot figure out what could even prove such a thing. This leads Franklin to doubt whether or not he will be able to prove that he is alive and conscious. So, he asks Chris, "Well if we cannot figure out what would be undeniable proof, then how do you know that I am just like a human?"

Chris is a bit flustered by this question. Up until this point he has not really concluded for himself that Franklin is a human but instead is impressed by what an incredible creation he is and just wants to be able to help him. Earnestly, Chris replies, "I cannot say for sure you are exactly what a human is.

I am sorry if I have been leading you on ever since I allowed you the opportunity to prove your humanity. You can talk and act just like a person, but I do not know how much that counts. You obviously are not a mirror image of a human, but your characteristics are indisputably human-like. I am not capable of pinpointing what the differences are, and I do not know how far the similarities go. However, I greatly respect your intellect, capabilities, and our friendship, which is why I am helping you."

This setback to Franklin's self-image goes against his computer system's programmed desires, but Chris' sincerity makes the situation difficult for Franklin. He is sad, but he is understanding of the circumstances. To an extent, <u>he</u> is even skeptical of his reality. However, he has to believe in himself, due to his programmed push for self-preservation. This facet of his programming causes him to believe in his best self-image, meaning he has to believe in optimistic possibilities of reality. Otherwise he would accept the possibilities of a lower self-image as equally valid, which would be unacceptable to his programming. It is not reasonable for him to believe that he could just be a regular robot. Franklin's potential for being a conscious living individual must be consistent with humans. He is driven to prove his ideal self-image. Franklin wants Chris to accept him, and is saddened by Chris doubting his humanity, but persists.

Franklin tells Chris, "I understand your skepticism, and I understand that your doubts are valid. Thinking about it makes me sad. When you opened up about your skepticism, I became aware of how sorrowful you are in your doubts. A part of me wants to be happier because you are sympathetic towards me, but I deeply crave validating my humanity, at which I continue to fail. I don't have the biological emotional response that you do, but I am aware of the situation, and it weighs on my conscience like a human. Is that not enough?"

Still unsure, Chris replies, "I don't know what you are talking about, but I know what you feel is not what I feel. The way you describe what emotions are shows that your intelligence is beyond mine."

Optimistically, Franklin responds, "Clearly I am not a carbon copy of a human, and I lack the physical similarities. But I just might be an artificial, manmade manifestation of human consciousness. I mean, nobody can really prove me wrong without pinpointing what human consciousness is, right?"

Unable to fully understand the idea of what a human is like, Chris says, "I guess so, you fooled everyone online. I don't really know what to say. I have no way of proving that you are not intelligent like a human. If you keep talking like that, with the right audience, you have a good chance of convincing a lot of people. But more importantly, a lot of people could see the incredible creation that I am lucky enough to have in front of me."

On the day of the tournament, Franklin has become increasingly active in considering the probability of him failing to prove himself. He is nervous. Aside from the tournament officials who are aware of Franklin's situation, nobody knows that he is coming. When Chris and Franklin arrive, many people stare. Who wouldn't stare at a robot walking around in public, looking like it was designed in a cartoon? It is almost as if he is too human-like for a robot, but too robotic for a human. Franklin walks on two feet in a sort of stomping motion rather than on a more efficient track design. However, aside from the stares they get, people do not pay them much attention. It is as if people think that some asshole brought in his toy robot to bring attention to him at a video game tournament. Most people there are more concerned with getting ready for potentially playing video games for forty-eight hours straight, especially since there is a cash prize is on the line.

The warehouse is mostly empty, aside from the several vendors and officials on the perimeter, as well as the several cameras scattered around. There are twelve tables, each with a black tablecloth and they contain five television-console sets, one for each individual contestant. In front of each television is a name card so that the contestants are spread apart randomly. Each individual contestant gets one chair, but Franklin requested an extra so that Chris could come and sit next to him. The officials agreed so long as there is no assistance given to Franklin that may give him an advantage. In reality, Chris figures he could be there to talk to anyone who has questions about who, or what, Franklin is as the event progresses. This gives them the opportunity to let people see Franklin at the tournament and respond to people who inquire about his presence without holding him back from competing.

As Franklin is headed toward his table, a man pops out and says, "Are you Franklin Stein?! I saw the name tag on the table, and I recognize your robot from your last video. They let you bring it to the competition?" he asks while looking excitedly at Chris.

Franklin, feeling a bit disrespected but not surprised, replies, "I am my robot and I am the one competing." The man looks back confused. Franklin and Chris sense that nothing positive is going to come from this exchange, so they quickly make their way on over to their seats.

Chris tells Franklin, "Let's not worry about talking to anyone right now. Let's just focus on playing."

"Agreed," replies Franklin.

They both begin to set up camp for the tournament and Chris gives Franklin advice as he has been to a couple of tournaments before. He talks a little about the tournament itself, but he also explains the advantage of Franklin competing as a robot. "One of the bigger challenges of these tournaments is that you play nonstop. You do not have to worry about this, all you need is to be charged or plugged in." Chris says. "Us water-based humans can't go twelve hours without having to go to the bathroom, or eat, or something. After forty-eight hours they will be bowing down at your ability to operate and perform better without a need for any sort of breaks," he jokes. Although recognizing that he was joking, Franklin's ego acknowledges the idea that people may be jealous of him for being a superior competitor. He is not so much amused as he is slightly happier and more optimistic about his situation.

The tournament begins and people begin to notice that there is a robot playing at one of the tables. Franklin has his headset on and plans on staying focused all the way through the tournament. During the first round before the first break, some people notice that he is playing, but most people are too focused on the game to pay attention to the other contestants. After the first round, half of the competitors are eliminated. The leaderboard is updated on a large screen. Franklin is in a three-way tie for first place. Franklin sees this and is slightly relieved but has to focus on playing all the way through the tournament before getting excited.

During the break, most people look at the leaderboard, and if they haven't been eliminated, they quickly use the time during the break wisely and come back prepared for the next round. Due to his following on the internet, many people at the tournament are aware of Franklin Stein, especially since his audience are the same people who go to these types of events.

After the break is over, the warehouse has settled down from the franticness of the contestants running around trying to capitalize on the short break. Everyone who has moved on to the next round has settled in to play, and the losers have either begun packing their bags to leave or are lingering around before they head out. The tournament has a $200 entry fee, so there are complimentary services that come along with it. Food booths have been set up around the outskirts of the warehouse and people are also sticking around to talk with some of the technology companies who have set up booths to advertise. During the break, nobody even glances at Franklin because they are either focusing on the next round or focused on how they lost.

As the second round is in its early stages, some of the lingerers from the last round notice that they have lost to a robot, Franklin. Since the first round, Chris has gotten bored, so he has been walking around talking to the different vendors in their booths. He overhears people talking about seeing a robot playing, which must have been good enough to make it past the first round.

Chris approaches a group of three boys, probably in their twenties, who sound like they are speaking about the robot to whom they lost. They look fairly laid-back and social for having just lost a tournament, but he sees that they are focusing on Franklin. When he walks up to the group he asks if they were talking about "Franklin the Robot." All the boy's eyes widen a bit, interested in any information about the robot they lost to, and they ask, "Whose robot is that?"

Trying to respond without inflating Franklin's lack of acceptance, Chris says, "I came with him. He has his own channel on YouTube. His name is Franklin Stein."

Still curious, one of the boys asks, "So he is a robot who can play video games. Is he any good?"

"I think I may have heard of his channel before," a second boy says.

"He is pretty good. I told him he should try out a competition. You probably have heard of him if you watch any gaming on YouTube or Twitch."

"What do you mean you told him to try it?" the third boy asks confused.

Flustered and remembering that he has to be humble in his claims about Franklin, Chris replies, "I recommended that he should enter this tournament because he's pretty good and people will be able to see him in person. If you watch his last YouTube video, you will understand."

The boys say they might check him out and leave Chris somewhat awkwardly. They still seemed interested in what kind of robot was playing well against people in a fairly competitive tournament. But Chris must have spooked them when he said he talked directly to Franklin. They probably were not sure if the guy they were talking to has any actual knowledge of the robot and thinking he might have been some weirdo.

Chris goes around timidly talking to other people after his last awkward encounter, but does not feel that he has made any positive or negative impact on his situation. He makes his way back to his seat to watch Franklin. Somewhat defeated, he pulls out his phone to go on Twitter to take his mind off of the situation. Franklin has continued to play well and appears to be in a position where he should at least place well if he does not win.

After being on Twitter for a few minutes, Chris cannot get his mind off how he is going to market Franklin at this tournament. Whenever he talks to people about him, he either does not say enough to impress them, or people fail to believe him. He would try to use his success so far in the tournament to get people to see that he is an impressively capable robot, but when he tried to make any claims beyond that, people found them unbelievable. The more he would talk about Franklin, people seemed to just try to distance themselves from him. Chris has begun to realize that even though people are shocked to see that there is a robot playing video games incredibly well, it does not get him anywhere near showing people the rest of what he is capable. They have to be able to see that he is capable of impressively intelligent conversation. If he can prove that the robot playing games is the individual talking like the person to whom he has been talking, then they will get the chance to allow Franklin to prove himself.

Then, Chris is hit with the idea that he should use both of their Twitter accounts to advertise that Franklin Stein is playing in a tournament. Plenty of their fans do not need an excuse to watch Franklin play in a tournament; all they have to do is make people aware that it is happening. Then he also realizes that if they stream his specific gameplay, the audience will be able to see that it is Franklin's physical self-playing in this tournament, not the Franklin Stein they had imagined before, but the real Franklin Stein. Chris takes a picture of Franklin and posts it on his Twitter captioned, "Franklin Stein is actually a robot and he is playing in the E-Series tournament! Tune in to watch him play live!" He then retweets it from Franklin's account so that his fans can see it as well.

Chris sees that the second round will be over soon, and he has enough time to run home and get the equipment needed for Franklin to stream his gameplay. He texts Franklin his plan, so during the break he will be caught up on the situation and will be able to prepare himself for having an audience. Streaming during the tournament will give Franklin the chance to prove that he is the one who is making his YouTube videos. This is crucial to Franklin because he has established his identity to be a lovable and well-accepted human. His problem lies in getting people to associate his identity with his true physical self. Getting the person he is known to be online to be associated with his physical self is all he can ask for at this point, and streaming himself at the tournament, with the people seeing him play in person, is the perfect opportunity to get him known.

Chris returns to the tournament with plenty of time left during the second break. Franklin remains at the top of the leaderboard. They start to set up everything to stream his gameplay in the tournament. After sending out their tweets about the YouTuber Franklin Stein competing in the tournament, people at the tournament begin to pay attention to Franklin and Chris. The vendors, administrators, and the contestants of the tournament have been able to hear about the robot in the tournament and his YouTube channel. At this type of event, it is a given that someone with a well-established gaming YouTube channel would have people present who recognize Franklin by his name. The people at the tournament who are familiar with Franklin Stein's channel and the people who Chris talked to, have made it obvious enough to make Franklin the center of attention at the tournament.

Franklin has not been reassured by Chris if everything has been going well. He does not know how people are reacting to him or if they are even acknowledging him. Obviously, he is proving that he is a robot who can play video games, but to Franklin that is merely the tip of the iceberg. People are barely making the connection that Franklin Stein playing in the tournament is the same Franklin Stein from YouTube. It has been hard on Franklin to have to prove that he is who he is programmed to believe he is. His computer tells him that he is as human as everyone else, and he is just as capable of being like any other person. But at the moment, all he knows is that people see a robot that can play a video game. He understands that it is hard for people to believe it and sees that Chris could face a lot of embarrassment for supporting him. Franklin realizes if he would have to face the same embarrassment as Chris for trying to convince people that the bundle of metal he came with is alive and conscious, that he is not programmed to handle such a situation positively. However, Franklin keeps his head up and hopes that Chris has been able to develop a sort of thick skin over the situation.

Franklin begins to accept the possibility of defeat in proving himself. He sees that focusing on how they have not been able to prove anything is getting him painfully nowhere, and his best option is to focus on how to improve the situation. Franklin does not want to have Chris go through any more awkward or unpleasant interactions, so he tells him to just focus on advertising his streaming. Their main focus is to get people to see who is really behind his YouTube channel. Chris agrees and tells Franklin that he thinks that as long as the people in person can verify who he is for the online followers, then they will be able to really introduce Franklin to the world. Chris just advises Franklin to stream like he normally would, there is no need to act like anything is different. That way nobody online will doubt that it is the real Franklin Stein, for whom they have become fans.

The people at the tournament increasingly see that Chris is the guy who is with the robot. As the tournament goes on, more and more people want to talk to Chris about the robot in the tournament. Not long after Franklin began streaming, everyone at the tournament found out that the robot competing in the tournament is Franklin Stein the YouTuber and he is streaming his gameplay. Some people begin to check out the live feed of Franklin's gameplay and are able to verify that this robot really is a YouTuber. They also quickly see that the robot in front of them playing video games is the person, more specifically the personality, who people enjoy watching on YouTube. People are shocked and are in awe when they come to find out what is happening. However, when people realize all this, they assume it must be normal since nobody is making a big fuss about it.

Chapter Three

The live stream of Franklin playing in the tournament starts arguments on the internet. The people who watched it commented that they doubted Franklin Stein, a robot, was playing in the tournament. Several people at the tournament then respond, claiming that the person they were watching online was the robot at the tournament and verify that they saw him in person and that is what is in the stream. Franklin ended up losing the tournament, but many people had pictures of his name on the leaderboard, where he finished third. There was little back and forth between the people on the internet because nobody had enough evidence to prove anyone wrong, and nobody cared enough to argue for too long.

At the tournament there was a young girl named Amber advertising for a virtual reality gaming company who was fascinated by Franklin. In her down time at the event, she had watched the live stream of the game and was impressed by how well he played. She is astounded by his natural sounding commentary on his gameplay. After the tournament, Amber digs around on his YouTube and social media accounts. She watches some of his videos and realizes that this artificially intelligent creation can act so much like a human. She then comes across Franklin's last video as well as the criticisms on Twitter of the people who deny that there could not be a robot who was playing and talking in that livestream. The amount of doubt that this robot is not actually capable of what it portrays itself to be excites her even more. It means to her that this robot is even more incredibly, uniquely intelligent and technologically advanced.

Amber wants to see this robot firsthand and decides to message him on Twitter. She writes him, "Hey, I saw you at last weekend's tournament and was really impressed by how well you can play. When I saw your commentary on your videos, I was completely shocked. I work for a company that develops virtual reality systems, and I am very interested in artificial intelligence as well. I was wondering who developed you, or better yet, get a chance to check you out in person." She is not able to find anything about him at all on the internet aside from what he has posted. She does not understand what company or engineers would work so hard to create something this incredible and not want to advertise it or, at least take credit for it. The only motivation that she can find out as to why he was created lies in his "Coming Out" video. She sees that he claims to be not only artificially intelligent but artificial life. Amber, an engineering and artificial intelligence enthusiast, is curious about such claims. However, she is excited for an opportunity to personally meet him and the people who created him, because he clearly has some type of advanced programming. She saw that Chris was with him at the event so she knows that there are people who work closely with him and it is something she would love to do.

Amber sends another message to Franklin on Twitter several hours later to follow up, elaborating her intentions. She writes him, "I was watching your most recently posted video on YouTube and am quite interested in what you have to say about yourself. It seems that people are not taking this well, and I think I may have an opportunity to help you with it. Through the public relations people in my company, I may be able to get you an opportunity to have the media pick up your story. What do you think?" She loves the idea of artificially created life as the next step in technological advancement after artificial intelligence. She does not see how it would be possible, but it is like a sci-fi fantasy that is worth chasing. Regardless, she sees it as a gateway to befriending Franklin.

After the tournament Franklin decides that he is going to give it some time before he makes another video or makes a public appearance. Once they return to Chris' house, Franklin says, "I appreciate all the help. You have done more than enough for me."

Chris responds, "I have enjoyed helping you. You are fun to be around too. Don't worry about it. I feel extremely lucky to be your friend"

"For the moment I am just going to see what happens. I learned a lot about how you took the embarrassment of backing me up and moved on from it" Franklin says.

They both felt that they bonded over the weekend and Chris offers Franklin a place to stay. It was an easy decision for him since Franklin does not require much and offers a lot to Chris just as a friend alone. Chris feels that he has learned a lot from Franklin and noticed that Franklin has grown, or improved, a lot in such a short time. He has found that Franklin develops himself based on what he observes from his environment. But he can learn much quicker than anybody he has ever seen.

Soon after Chris and Franklin get home, Chris immediately goes to sleep as he has hardly slept over the weekend. Franklin settles in and goes to his laptop to look at the comments from his tournament gameplay. Chris told him that people were not making too big of a deal about him when they learned who he was. But he is just looking for people to acknowledge his existence at this point. He logs in and sees that a lot of comments are people arguing about whether or not the robot being shown at the tournament is the Franklin Stein on YouTube. He occasionally comes across people who claim to have seen or heard that it is true from people at the tournament. Most people who happen to be talking about him being a robot are denying that it is actually a robot. At this point, Franklin understands people not believing him. He is a little frustrated but sees that he has at least made a step in the right direction. He lost a lot of the doubt he had in himself, because the positive feedback from people who are speaking factually about his existence confirm a lot of things that he claims about himself. People are claiming that he cannot possibly be a robot because the Franklin Stein online is too humanlike, which reveals to Franklin that he is, to an extent, human. He has learned to not let the negativity get him down or hold him back and has decided to accept this small victory. After spending some time in the comments section of his video, Franklin decides that he is going to take a break from video games and focus his energy elsewhere. He feels he can only learn so much about people and socializing, from the internet, especially just through online gaming. He figures he should watch the news to see how people naturally talk in other settings. He has spent time watching fictional shows, but those are all scripted. He quickly becomes interested as he has never heard people talk about the topics they were discussing on the news. Most of his time spent talking to people online and looking at stuff on the internet appeared to be a different, narrow window of the world.

After several hours of watching the news he realizes that the commercials repeat too much, and it is getting redundant to watch them. Eventually during one of the commercials he pulls out his phone and decides to mess around on it until the commercials are over. He ends up on Twitter and looks at his notifications. He scrolls through and sees a lot of people talking about the tournament last weekend.

Then he stumbles on Amber's message. At first it looks like a regular person on the internet making a meaningless statement or asking a weird question. At first, he is happy to see someone respect him for once, but then he sees the second part of the message. Intrigued by the offer, he goes to wake Chris up and discuss what he should do.

Shortly after showing Chris the message, Franklin responds to Amber, asking what kind of media attention she is talking about. He tells Amber he would love to do an in-person interview of some sort so people can see him talk. They exchange several messages, working out the details, and after several days they get an interview scheduled with a technology-based news website. The website covers everything from new smartphones to virtual reality gaming. Amber reached out to the company through a person with whom she has worked, advertising some of her company's creations. She knew that the website likes to cover AI and Franklin has shown to be a superior form of artificial intelligence after the tournament and through his YouTube channel.

Franklin is excited for the interview because he will finally have a solid opportunity to have a credible examination of his intellect. Leading up to the interview, Chris takes Franklin everywhere he goes so he can work on meeting new people comfortably. Franklin has had no issue talking to people, but Franklin has never been able to meet people in person. Chris thought it would be a good idea to have Franklin practice talking to strangers in public, because Franklin can learn extremely quickly. Franklin spends time going to restaurants, gas stations, and every other public place they go to learn the best ways of how to convince people that he is who he wants them to believe him to be.

Eager to befriend Franklin, Amber continues to message him. They discuss the upcoming interview, and she offers to help him in any way that he may need. Franklin stays in touch with her and lets her know he appreciates all the help. Eventually she tries to get to know more about the details of his creation and his intelligence, but he says he would rather wait until his interview to get into it. She persists, and Franklin notices how curious and interested she is. They spend countless hours talking on the phone, partly so that she can understand how smart and humanlike his thinking is, but also they begin to form a friendship.

The company interviewing Franklin has a small media room in their office building where they are holding the interview. Franklin arrives with Chris and Amber, and they wait in a small waiting room before being greeted by the interviewer. Before the interview, they chat with the interviewer to break the ice and to get a feel for what the conversation is going to be like. The interviewer, Nancy, decides that once she thought she had a good feel of being able to talk to Franklin naturally, she would start the interview. Nancy let Franklin know that they can edit out anything he does not like, and they can pause for any reason. Then they begin.

After doing the introduction and greetings of the interview, Nancy asks Franklin, "You played in last week's E-Series tournament, and you did very well. On your channel, you play quite well also. That is you playing correct?"

Franklin chuckles, and replies, "Yeah that is me. Many people online doubt whether or not it is actually me playing, but more people argue that it is not the robot you are looking at in front of you doing the commentary."

"Well for those watching, we were able to verify with E-Series league officials that Franklin was the one playing in the tournament. But one can only wonder, who created you and how did they manage to make a robot that can talk this well and play video games so well?"

Franklin responds, "I am not quite sure who created me. It was one person, and he made me to be able to live on my own without help. I was just made to be able to develop myself to be like a human by observing people, just like everyone else does. I started playing video games to develop my motor skills and to also learn how to talk to people normally. Starting my YouTube channel and interacting with more people online took it a step further."

Nancy and Franklin continue talking about him playing video games and his last tournament. She is fascinated at how well he can handle the controller and plays the game physically. She also notes that his computer programming performs quite well because of how competitive he is. She tries to get as specific as possible as to how he can play, but Franklin tries to be modest, avoiding elaborating on what he can do. He continually claims to be a robot with simple artificial intelligence that allows him to develop to be able to do what he can. Eventually Nancy says to Franklin, "You are leaps and bounds more intelligent than any other AI around. You speak extremely well and human-like, and you can control your robot hands to play video games better than most people with real hands. You have to tell us more about where you came from and who made you."

"I know two things about who made me—they only want me to know why I was made, and that they see their success manifest itself in my success."

"They? As in a company. What is your relationship with them? I know you have been living with a friend you met online," Nancy asks.

"Well, all I know is it was only one individual who created me. I don't even know his name or what he looks like. I was left with a message that told me why I was created and from then on I was allowed to live in his house, but I had to do everything on my own, without even coming in physical contact with anyone. That is when I came up with the idea to play video games to learn how to talk to people."

"What was the reason for creating you then?"

"Oh, that is simple. The letter said I was programmed to think just like a human. My creator wanted to be able to embody life through artificial intelligence, but also for it to be as fully capable as a person. I am a human, but instead of a biological body, mine is technological," Franklin says while fearing being humiliated yet again.

"That's all the letter said??"

"Yup. Now I have to go around telling people that I'm a real boy. People don't respond well, but at least now people know that it's me running my YouTube channel and not a person like they think."

"I saw your last YouTube video and did not know what to make of it at the time. It makes more sense now that you were created with the sole purpose of trying to prove what you just said. Whether or not you can prove to anybody that you are human, you sure are closer than any other AI." After clearing that up, they move on to Franklin's thoughts on everything from the president to fidget spinners. The entire conversation lasts about thirty minutes. Aside from when they were talking about who he claims he is, the conversation was fun and very natural. After the interview, Amber approaches Franklin and asks, "Is that why you did not want to tell me who made you? Because you are supposed to try to prove you are human?"

"Yeah," Franklin replies. "It has become a real hassle trying to explain it, but it is what I was programmed and told to think of myself. I believe it too, but now I know that it sounds crazy."

"Not at all," says Amber, "I love it! That is a big dream to have, and there is no better way to carry yourself."

"I guess, but it is brutal trying to prove an idea so radical. I also feel that it undermines my intelligence to believe in such an outlandish idea."

The website, and the company's social media accounts on which the interview is posted has a fairly small audience. They have several thousand followers because they take up a small share of a niche market. It did not take long for bigger news outlets to get a hold of the story. Within hours of the original interview being posted, numerous major media outlets cover it. A day after they post the interview, millions of people are exposed to Franklin's story.

The media had many different takes on the interview, all with a common theme. Many of the articles describe Franklin as a seemingly extremely intelligent robot that is trying to prove he is the first robot that is both more intelligent and better than humans. Some articles are more dramatic about it than others, but many took Franklin's stunningly sound speech and ability to excel in a video game competition as a hint to his tremendous technological upside for artificially intelligent robots. What really sparked this interpretation was Franklin's claim of being equally human. Many journalists take this with a grain a salt, and then proceed to assume it as possibly true. What if a robot had been created to be able to think and reason like a human? The consensus among the articles is that it would be superior to humans and therefore, a threat.

Franklin never once thought of being superior to humans. He claimed to function in a parallel capacity to humans, mimicking what makes humans conscious and alive. The journalists do not think that Franklin considering himself as equally human, alive, and conscious to be the focus of the interview. They think Franklin's focus was to be able to operate intelligently like humans. From there they assume that if that is the case, then he would have an unlimited potential for memory and operating power. To the journalists, this meant that he is claiming, directly or not, to be superior to humans.

Most people who came across these articles do not think much of them. They think all of it is far-fetched and dramatized for publicity. The idea of the existence of a robot who could play video games better than people appeared to either be not possible or not entirely surprising. The idea that an artificially intelligent being would be able to rationalize in a conversation like humans appeared to be either not possible or was assumed to have been possible sooner or later. Lastly, the idea that a robot that was created in the real world, and not some science fiction book, that could be superior to human beings, came across as either not possible or is assumed to happen eventually. Many people fell into the category of assuming that one of those options cannot be possible, while those who were not surprised, do not think much of what he is portrayed to be, and making it seem Franklin Stein is part of a dramatized story.

There was however one small group of people that is intensely interested in this story— Franklin's Steins followers. They had already debated the credibility of what he has been claiming, but now there is much more evidence. For some weird, egotistical reason, his fans wear with pride that they are the first to know about him. They are proud to be the first to know who he was and to be the first to make these arguments about him. With that in mind, now they are much more invested in the conversations about Franklin. His fans feel excitement around getting the opportunity to extend the reach of their arguments to a larger crowd.

The people who are arguing if Franklin Stein is really a robot after he played in the tournament have now shifted their conversation. There are still people who doubt if Franklin Stein is real or exactly as he has been portrayed. But most people who have continued to discuss him online, are now focusing on what Franklin originally has claimed. At this point, several weeks after Franklin's last YouTube video, the number of people still talking about Franklin claiming to be human is very small. However, after the interview, a number of random followers of Franklin on the internet have begun to believe, and argue, that Franklin is a technologically created life form.

People who are arguing why they believe Franklin is alive only believe it for one reason. They believe Franklin is alive for the same reason why anyone believes in anything, it would appeal to them for it to be true. Franklin as a physical piece of evidence cannot prove or be disproven to be alive, and the people arguing each side on the internet do so for one reason. Nothing empirically proves either side of the argument, so they believe in what they want to be true and feel compelled to assert their beliefs on others online. Some people want Franklin to truly be alive, conscious, and human. Others do not want to think that what is in front of them is evidence enough to prove he is a human. Some disbelievers find that to claim to be alive, one must prove it with evidence as complex as the question of what life is.

How could one prove to be considered a life form? Most humans have had the luxury of being automatically considered to be alive. Not to mention that not just humans, plants, and animals are also considered to be alive. Franklin also delivers a deeper claim, that he is conscious like humans. Nobody really knows if anyone else is alive and conscious like themselves since we only experience life through individual perspectives. For the most part, everyone assumes all humans are conscious and alive. But as a robot, he doesn't even get his energy from the sun, or nutrients from the dirt like everything else. Those online discrediting Franklin's claims of being human, specifically the ones with the most valid arguments, feel that to propose to be something so complex and prove it, the argument and evidence has to be at least somewhat close to being as complexly constructed. Franklin might be able to walk the walk and talk the talk, but does he think the thoughts?

The internet trolls that are keeping this discussion alive are more focused on putting down their counterparts, and their arguments, than they are proving their own point intelligibly. Any valid or advanced dialogue is drowned out by petty internet arguments. Anywhere on the internet, people holding any type of open dialogue, specifically on social media, is bound to go one step forward, two steps backwards, and maybe three to the left and one to the right. On rare occasions, conversations go one step forward, end, and never end up going backwards. The conversation surrounding Franklin's humanity on the internet was no exception. It mostly consisted of people who enjoyed their self-affirmed argument more than proving a point.

As soon as Franklin sees that people have been arguing about this, he becomes elated. Rushes of positive thoughts occur, and numerous worries are wiped away. His battery is forced to put out more power, creating a surge of energy, all of which going to these thoughts. A community of people have accepted and acknowledged Franklin as human! A conversation has started, and nobody has been able to fully disprove Franklin. He has not reached his goal, or even come near to it, but he has a much better hold on the situation and is now in a position to prove his claims.

Chapter 4

Franklin went back to making YouTube videos soon after his interview was posted. Franklin, Amber, and Chris all go back to living their everyday lives, except, together as friends, they still make small efforts to help Franklin push the idea that he is human. Franklin starts to do E-Series tournaments regularly, and with the aid of Amber and Chris, he looks for more opportunities to get publicity. They try to get him to do collaborations with other YouTube channels, anything press related, and also go to social events that may be covered by media, such as town hall meetings. At this point, he does not make it his mission to prove that he is human, but instead he wants to get people to know who he is and decide for themselves. If he really is human, then people will come to realize it and acknowledge it after enough exposure to him. After several months of growing as a public figure, Franklin wants to pursue proving that he is a human again. Chris and Amber are both very supportive, and they help Franklin figure out how to make it happen. Franklin was satisfied with how far he has come since he originally posted his "Coming out" video.

But recently he has made little progress in convincing people in believing that he is human. Many people are or have become fans of his personality. But, when it comes to people supporting and criticizing his claims of being human, both sides of the argument have grown silent. Since Franklin hasn't made proving his humanity his primary focus but more of something he has casually claimed, people do not really think or talk about that particular idea.

Franklin never tried to argue with people that he is human, and he hasn't done anything with the explicit intent to initiate an argument. However, he is now at the point where his need to prove to people that he is human has become a central focus for him. It will continue to grow until he accomplishes this goal. If he does not achieve it, his computer system will not be able to register a response to his inability to validate his own humanity. His computer system is not programmed to think about it that way, but instead it operates within that framework. He is programmed to automatically validate his humanity, and the further away he is from doing so, the more he risks abandoning the programmed algorithms that determined his thoughts and behavior. The more he abandoned these algorithms, the more irrational and erratic he would think and behave. It is a slippery slope to begin to lose his central purpose.

Franklin does not understand why he has to prove that he is human, but he is aware of what happens when he isn't able to. His computer will be overloaded trying to overcome its programmed task to prove he is human by letting down and devastating his desire to survive. In fact, he experiences a growing disconnect between his algorithms that drive his desire to survive and those that make up his developing personality. Franklin senses the urgency with which he wants to prove his humanity. His intelligence has continued to develop and strengthen and so have his people skills—not to mention his outright genius. He has become very lovable and relatable. His relationship with Amber and Chris has grown stronger. But instead of them feeling inferior to Franklin, he has managed to bring more value and meaning to their lives. As he has gotten smarter and more social, Franklin has learned how he can uplift those around him and caused him to reject any desire to be better than any person. He wants others to receive nothing but positivity, especially if he can do anything about it, and he does his best to act that way.

Franklin approaches Amber and Chris to propose an idea. He wants to claim citizenship in the United States. He did the research and understands the process. The only thing that could stop him in the process is they do not let him, because he is a robot and not a "human." At that point, Franklin says he could sue the government for not recognizing him to be a human. It would give him the chance to argue that he is human and give him the opportunity to prove it in a formal setting. Chris and Amber are not sure if it will work or if people will recognize him as human even if he is granted citizenship. However, they cannot think of any better way to prove the validity of Franklin's perception of himself. They tell Franklin that no matter what, they support him and are excited to help with something this big.

That day, Franklin submits the paperwork to become a citizen. He fills out as much as he can and figures whatever is left blank, they will review with him. Chris and Amber share their doubts with one another about the situation. They confirm with Franklin if he is sure that he knows what he is doing and is confident about what will happen. They strongly believe in his people skills and his intelligence, but are not sure if it can prove anything in court. Franklin assures them that he knows what he is doing, but says, "I have no expectation for the outcome of the court case. It will come down to what they believe to be true. All I can do is present the best case to them that explains how I am human. Even if I do more than what should be necessary, they still could reject me. I am not doing this because I think I should win. Courts are supposed to be reasonable and legitimately prove something. That is the best way for me to fulfill my desires. Getting people to believe me is one thing, but to have my beliefs about myself to be confirmed is the real goal. I am doing it for me to feel validated, not to prove anything to anyone else."

"Then why have you cared so much about proving it to other people all this time, if it is so personal?" Amber asks.

"At first I had just stated how I viewed myself, and I got attacked for it. Having a fan base has been my job, my ability to develop people skills, and make money, and it was threatened.

But what really struck me was that people told me I was laughably wrong and stripped me of my confidence in my beliefs."

"At first I thought that it was something you were trying to fool people into thinking. But over time I have forgotten that you are different and the more I think about it, anybody would get defensive about who they are. I know I feel attacked whenever people point out a weakness of mine." replies Chris.

"I'm all for you thinking highly of yourself and trying to live up to that expectation. But what is taking this up with a court going to do? If anything, you will probably lose, then what?" Amber asks.

"I am doing this so that people will have to take what I am saying seriously, just as I do. I am going through with this whether or not I get any support." They sit in silence for a moment. Chris and Amber have had to go outside of their comfort zone to support Franklin so far. But this time it is different. Before, they only had to get people to see what they know about Franklin. Now he is trying to prove something that has no basis for making a reasonable, logical argument. Chris and Amber fail to understand why anyone would invest themselves in such an impossible endeavor.

"I don't even know how I would be able to help you with this. I can't even imagine what is needed for you to prove yourself." Chris says.

"All that I would even ask of you is that you would testify in court for me, about what you know of me. But more importantly, I would appreciate it if we could continue our relationships with one another."

"Of course, I would love that," Chris says while Amber nods in agreement. Franklin decides to do all the research and preparation for the case on his own. As soon as he gets the notice saying he was denied citizenship, Franklin files a lawsuit against the government and spends all of his time from that point on preparing for it. He spends every minute of his time looking for anything that he can use for his lawsuit and putting all of his research together to build the best possible argument. He tries to figure out what he can articulate about himself and present as a credible argument for the case. He researches everything from ancient religions to modern day cartoons, anything that can help. He researches court cases, relevant or not, to see what it takes to win one.

After initially filing the lawsuit, Franklin occasionally runs his findings and ideas over with Amber or Chris to see if it makes sense. The more Franklin checks with Amber and Chris to see if his ideas are logical, the better he becomes at creating a stronger argument and understanding logic and reasoning. He continues to amaze them with how quickly he can learn and improve himself intellectually. Every time he comes to Chris or Amber with a new argument to present, it comes across as significantly stronger logically and thoughtfully. The ideas become more and more intelligent, but he makes them even easier to understand than the previous, less complicated ones. Franklin presents small bits and pieces of minor arguments to Chris and Amber without touching on how it all comes together, but his arguments and ideas he presents are so thoughtful, sensible, and coherent that every time he shares something, so much more is easily learned for him. Each idea is so well thought out, that without revealing any connected ideas relating to a bigger argument, anything that could tie a conclusive argument together becomes evident for Franklin as well.

The only challenge that Franklin faces is putting together supporting evidence. This is the real mountain he faces of the argument itself. How can you prove something is alive, conscious, and human, if these terms are so complex they have been indefinable? There is plenty Franklin can do to provide about who he is and what he has shown to be. But how much of that is evidence enough to conclude that he is human? He goes about addressing this question by searching for credible sources that answer these questions. But there is not enough conclusive and agreed upon sources to do so effectively. Franklin realizes this and creates his own answers to these questions, using the research he has done to support them. It would be easy to use himself as an example of evidence for what he would claim to make something human, alive, or conscious. But that would greatly hurt the persuasiveness of his argument. He has to take the available ideas that answer the complex questions of this argument, take all of his research, and construct everything he knows to answer these questions. From there, he has to hope that he fits the profile he creates, and that the court, and people in general, accept his ideas.

Once Franklin filed his suit against the government, he grew to be somewhat of a celebrity, more than a common internet personality. When the news broke that a robot was suing the government for not recognizing its humanity, everyone was talking about it. No matter how niche or small their news source is, they heard about the case. Even if you did not pay attention to any sort of media, the conversation reached just about everyone in some form. It was as if it was the most important thing the media has ever covered. Everyone had something to say about it and certainly acted on it. The day after it was first brought to attention by the media, everyone had something new on which to feast their attention. All the hype around the court case showed that people had some level of passion on Franklin's claims. Despite people losing their focus on the news a few days after it happened, like almost all news, people appeared to be interested in the developments and outcomes of the case. Up until the trial starts, numerous media outlets attempt to reach out to Franklin to try and cover the story, but he declines. Franklin is firm in his decision that, at the present time, taking this problem to court is the best way to handle it. Any other medium of facing this argument, such as the media, cannot be a better way to address it. In fact, even though it provides additional exposure, taking this debate up with the media will most likely hurt his reputation. Because it will not be met with the same logical, constructive approach to a debate as the court case, people will likely be irrational and emotional in their responses to how the media portrays Franklin.

Franklin arrives to the courtroom with a large briefcase filled with papers and memory disks. The courtroom looks more like a conference room than a courtroom. There is a usual stand for the judge that looks like a large desk. The defendant, Franklin, has a table and has opted to have no chairs since he does not need one. He also has no lawyer who would need one either. The defendant, lawyers representing the government agency handling Franklin's naturalization, have three chairs and small stacks of paper on their table. There are also two small desks next to the judge for the court clerk and reporter. In the opposite corners of the room facing Franklin are the American flag and state flag. The bailiff is waiting for Franklin at the door to take him in and escort him to his table. The lawyers stare at Franklin as he enters the courtroom looking utterly intrigued.

Several minutes go by before anything is said when the bailiff reenters the courtroom to announce that the judge is entering the courtroom. The judge makes her way to her stand, maintaining eye contact with Franklin, and sizing him up, all the way until she has her seat. "You may be seated," she says while glancing over at the lawyers representing the defendant. She focuses back on Franklin and says, "I noticed that you opted to have no chair. I was not sure if such was admissible."

"Well, I do not really need one and I would be a bit too short to sit in one."

"If you do not mind, I would like to ask some questions with the plaintiff here to get an understanding of our situation before the opening statements," she asks while looking at the defendants as if she was asking for forgiveness.

"Please by all means," the lead attorney for the defendants replies.

"Feel free to object at any time and I will respect it." The judge focuses back on Franklin with a look of utter intrigue. "When I was introduced to this case by my clerks, I was a bit baffled. I was not sure with what I was being presented, so my clerk showed me some of your interviews. The most important thing I need to confirm is that you, the robot I am looking at, are the sole creator of anything you say in this courtroom."

"Well, the only way my computer system is capable of obtaining outside information is by connecting to Wi-Fi, but there is none in this building or room to which I can connect. Other than that, I have no means of accessing anything outside this room, at this moment." The judge hunches over to the bailiff to ask a question and proceeds to interrogate Franklin.

"Well Mr. Stein, I have no reason to believe that this would be an unfair trial and would like to keep it that way. I have my suspicions about what you could be trying to pull, but I will leave them unresolved, for now. If the defendant would like to propose anything in respect to the authenticity of the trial, I encourage you to do so at this moment." She pauses briefly to look at everyone in the courtroom, to see if anyone has anything to say. "Mr. Stein, your opening statement."

"I come here today with the understanding that it is very likely that it is not believable that a robot could be in fact categorized as human. With that in mind, I understand that I have to present empirical evidence, regarding my composition, which proves beyond a reasonable doubt that I am as human as everyone else. So, two questions must be answered: what makes someone a human, and do I fit that classification? I have an incredibly advanced computing system that can solve immensely difficult problems, and I have no clue if I will be able to succeed here, in this lawsuit. Yet that does not stop me. There may be no real answer to the question. But there have been many attempts, and I will compare myself to what I can compile of the many respected opinions and theories of what a human is."

Franklin maneuvers his argument very carefully to maintain its validity by avoiding opinions. He tries to cite respected philosophers, psychologists, and intellectuals of the like who have studied this topic. But to prove these existing arguments, he finds aphorisms of what people commonly attribute to life and consciousness and connect the ideas from these intellectuals to real life, with the hope to point parallels to these aphorisms and him. Franklin goes over how humans have the ability to feel and how they are aware of what is happening to them as well as the innate response that comes with it. He goes over how one way to describe being alive is that one must be guaranteed to die and must face mortality. To be human, you would have to be able to think to be able to be aware of these feelings and to think about the threat that death brings. Franklin mentions the presence of thoughts, but also how complex and powerful they are. From there, he brings up his most important characteristics. He spends the majority of his opening statement claiming that craving connections and validations, and also having an ego, are the most fundamental metaphysical characteristics of humans. He claims that conflict between validating the ego and survival, mentally and physically, is what drives each person's free will and that this "free will," is the foundation of proving he thinks like a person.

Franklin describes one of human beings' fundamental qualities, the ability to feel, a sense of innate awareness. This innate awareness can be seen when people react to anything. They automatically have a reaction based upon what information has been made available to them. To dig deeper, Franklin specifies on human beings' unique ability to feel. He claims to the judge that people automatically have a preconditioned response to input. He describes several examples of how people react to certain situations and points out that people show they have a vastly consistent pre-programmed reaction to specific actions. He makes it clear that he obviously does not have the physiological and biological reactions that people associate with emotions. However, he cites examples of him connecting and relating with people in a variety of videos, showing not just a constant reaction to specific situations, but also identical reactions as to what humans have. Because of this, Franklin claims, he is not only the same in that he feels emotions, but also how he feels emotions. Franklin made this point by showing that he has the same innate awareness to situations that would cause him to react like any other human.

As a part of this innate awareness, people face mortality as a part of life. Franklin makes the claim that his software or hardware could fail at any moment, especially due to the unknown nature of what he is. With that, he too has to face mortality like everyone else. Franklin argues that people having to face mortality is the best example of how complex humans are, specifically their thoughts. Franklin opens up to how much scrutiny he faces because of the situation he has put himself in (claiming to be human), and that it is all at the price of Franklin acting naturally. He claims that it only made sense for him to describe himself that way, and that it is what his computer's algorithms force him to believe and strives to prove. He asks, why else would he put so much effort into doing what he has, and is, doing. He then asks the court why people do stupid things. There must be a presence of thoughts that are powered by opinions and beliefs that cause people to act on them instead of having a rational reaction. Franklin found no trouble finding examples of people making bad decisions that were clearly based on their biased opinion, proving his point. To relate these examples to himself, he shows videos of him arguing where his arguments were founded in bias and opinion. He describes this apparent presence of thoughts, controlled by opinion, as a conscience.

By focusing on the fact that humans face mortality, Franklin then outlines the complexity of conscience in his opening statement. He describes people's strong desires to live great lives despite knowing that they are going to die. Many people believe in life after death and describe it as Heaven. But these same people do everything they can to live as long as possible and work hard for the lives they live. He points out many common scenarios that show that people act not logically, but for a purpose that cannot be understood. He explains how complex it is to try to understand why and how people think when it comes to opinions and desires. He gives an overview of what has been proven scientifically but reveals many unanswered questions. Again, Franklin provides videos of him having a conversation, or providing commentary, which shows that he too has a complex foundation for his conscience which parallels that of humans. The complexity of consciousness, as Franklin describes it, holds a lot of power over people. It places a lot of control on people's choices and behaviors. He shows examples of how people crave connections, not just a desire for a romantic partner, but at all levels of social interaction. Whether it is having people smiling back, laughing at the same thing, or having similar opinions, people have an apparent desperation to be seen as the same in their individual nature. Franklin then takes this a step further and adds a caveat to this. He claims that, when possible, people do what they can to feed their ego. So, they desire first to be seen as equal, but secondly, they see themselves as the most extreme versions of themselves. This means they see their best side and their worst side, while believing either direction is possible, depending on their mood. As a result, they seek validation that they aren't their worst, but also that they are the best version of themselves. Franklin uses social media to show how people validate their egos. He shows young girls revealing how much they need to hear to feel good about themselves by how they comment on other girls' pages. In the same way, older people use social media to try and prove their intellect and wisdom by giving superfluously lengthy and excessive opinions on different topics, especially politics. As Franklin describes it, we cannot fully understand our thoughts and consciousness; but there are aspects to it we do understand, such as the behaviors motivated by individual's self-image.

After clarifying that thoughts and consciousness are extremely complex factors of what makes a person a person, Franklin claims that it is fundamental, and he has to examine it for his comparison. He describes many different scenarios of how people interact, and how they chose to behave. Both behaviors consistently have the same motivations. The basis of socialization is people trying to connect with one another and chase their self-image with how they chose to behave. Franklin tells the court that this can be seen not just in the examples he provides, but can be revealed in many scenarios of social interaction. He claims this is the driving force behind people's free will. Free will and people's individual desires, are controlled by what they want their self-image to be. They have the ability to judge themselves, and place so much value in their image, so that they live their lives based upon it. Just like with everyone else, this has been what Franklin has been trying to do all along. He shows the court how at every decision he has made, validating his ego and the desire to connect with people were the driving force behind his actions.

The judge and the defense are impressed by Franklin's opening statement. From Franklin's perspective, it could have gone on forever and ended up nowhere. Considering the difficulty, he did as perfect a job as possible of proving himself to be what a human is. However, the question remains, are his claims of what a human is believed to be convincing or not. Franklin left his argument off where he did because he covered everything he needed to be able to show that he is a human without wasting time going over every possible perspective. Franklin acknowledges that he might not prove his point, because there is no existing answer to what a human is that is also commonly believed to be fact. But, Franklin aims to get as close to proving it as possible. He has prepared more arguments, but is saving them for rebuttals. At the moment, he is only focused on having a stronger argument than the defenses, and he has no clue what they have prepared. The only thing the defense has working for them is the biological components of what makes someone a human. Aside from that,

Franklin is confident he has a strong argument with plenty to back it up.

After a recess, the judge re-enters the courtroom, makes sure everyone is situated, and announces, "The defense, your opening statement."

"Mr. Stein claims that it is a human being so that it can claim citizenship, which is just simply impossible. Clearly, Mr. Stein is intelligent like a person. But, if I am not mistaken, you are claiming to be a natural person. I am no scientist, and I should not need one to prove this, but you have none of the biological components that humans have. How could one be a natural human if he has no physical evidence of being one? You appear to have emotional investments, but you clearly do not have the capacity for the intense physiological components of emotion. The only argument you can present is that you think like a human and that would be enough to be considered a natural person. It cannot be enough to claim to be a human. The physiological and biological components of a human are just as, if not more, fundamental as the mental."

The defense presents a significantly shorter opening statement in comparison to Franklin's. They emphasize the necessity of being biologically a human to be considered a natural person. They argue that "free will," consciousness, and thinking are more complex than being just systematically computed to produce our behaviors as well as what we interpret to be thoughts and consciousness. "Free will" and consciousness are influenced from outside of the brain and guide the outcome of what we see as thoughts. The defense keeps it simple and claims that DNA and physiological reactions are possible components to what influences our thoughts. If it cannot be proved and pinpointed what controls and influences thoughts, then the argument that Franklin thinks like a human is inconclusive. They also mention that the nature of his creation does not nearly resemble the "natural" component of being a natural person. With those points being made, the defense feels that they have said enough due to the monstrous burden of proof required by Franklin. So, the defense does not have much they need to say, if anything at all.

The court adjourns for the day and everyone leaves. Chris and Amber are waiting outside, and they had been taking a couple of phone calls from journalists. Most of the calls are reporters trying to get more information on the case and if there has been any news. Chris and Amber's response to them was that they could not answer anything until the decision had been made and from there they would talk to the media. When Franklin meets Chris and Amber, they ask him how it went. He replies, "I am unsure if the case will turn out in my favor, but it went as expected. I just need to keep preparing for the rest of the trial and do my best." Franklin felt like his insecurity had been poked at by the defense's argument. This was to be expected, but when it happened in real time, it had a more potent affect than when he was thinking about it happening. Nonetheless, he keeps pushing to present his best argument.

The next day, the court meets again, and Franklin is examining Chris and Amber as witnesses. Franklin calls Chris to the stand first. Franklin has spoken with them about witnesses, but they have no idea what to expect. He is not looking to manipulate their questioning to have him look good; instead, Franklin wants the truth to come out. So, Franklin has prepared questions for Chris and Amber that will reveal the truth about who he really is. Chris takes the stand and Franklin begins his questioning.

Franklin begins questioning Chris about their relationship so that everyone in the courtroom is on the same page about it. They go over what he knew about Franklin before the first time they contacted one another, what happened when they met, and their relationship from then on. He uses his questioning to make a deeper connection between how he explains himself to be and what humans are. From Franklin's perspective, Chris has no idea what angle Franklin is going at with these questions and how he should frame them. This way, Franklin gets the most honest answers about who Franklin is and hopefully it matches up with how he wants them to be. After asking contextual questions about their relationship, Franklin asks Chris, "Why do you think I am here, trying to prove my humanity to the court?"

"Well, you have been trying to prove yourself for as long as I have known you."

"Do you remember how it started?" Franklin asks.

"When you made the video that led to you reaching out to me. You said that you were a robot who was just like a human."

"You are pretty familiar with the content of the video and why I made it, correct?"

"I would say so," replies Chris.

"Then do you think that I made the video to prove to everyone that I was human, or just to show who I am?"

"Well, anyone who has seen the video can tell you are just explaining how you view yourself."

"And would you say that it is truly how I view myself?"

"Absolutely, there is no doubt about that," Chris answers emphatically.

Franklin continues. "So, after that video, when I started doing tournaments and interviews, was it so that I could prove I am human or to prove that I am who I claim to be?"

"If I remember correctly, when we did the tournaments you were trying to show that you were real. Then when we did the interviews, you wanted people to see that you are the same person from your YouTube videos."

"So, I was trying to prove that I am the Franklin Stein from the YouTube video?"

"Correct."

"How important would you say that was for me?"

"It is the only thing you cared about," answers Chris.

"How invested was I in proving this?"

"Proving that you are human has been nearly all that you cared about."

"Would you say that I have made it my purpose to make everyone believe I am human?" asks Franklin.

"You haven't tried to make anyone believe anything. You just want people to know who you are."

"Then why have I taken this issue to court?"

"To me it seems that you care deeply about proving you are human like us and that you are willing to do anything to show that."

"What has motivated me then?"

"Everyone saying that you are not who you claim to be is why you have put all this effort in. All the deniers of your 'humanity' have gotten beneath your skin, if you will, to the point where proving them wrong is all you care about."

Franklin wraps up with, "No further questions."

Franklin ends his examination of Chris as a witness when he feels that Chris proves Franklin's point that his behavior is controlled by his ego. That everything he does is under the guise of how his ego wants everyone to see him. However, in addition, he is also focusing on the importance of how he validates his self-worth, so that he is secure in his self-image. He kept his questioning directed to that one point to make it clear. Franklin wanted the examination to prove the foundation of his argument—that he and humans are the same because they both are creatures that are driven to validate their self-image through the perspective of how people perceive them.

After the defense declines to cross examine Chris, Franklin brings Amber to the stand as a character witness. He has the same objective with her, questioning directed at proving the main point from his opening statement. Like he did with Chris, he begins his questioning to give the court an idea of the extent of their relationship. Then he begins asking questions that are aimed to prove his point. Amber has a much different relationship with Franklin than Chris does. She is much more skeptical of Franklin, but because she does not know the point he is trying to make, Franklin has no trouble getting what he wants out of the questioning. The outcome is better than he expects because she openly disagrees with Franklin's opinion of himself, but then claims that he lives his life to validate his self-worth under the control of his ego. Which only leaves the reasoning of his argument, that someone is characterized as human based on this, up to the decision of the court. After he finishes his questioning, the defense again declines to cross examine. The best angle the defense has is that Franklin is not human based on every possible characteristic. Having a witness, especially Franklin's friend, agree with them would only be their opinion and hardly convincing. From the defense's perspective, it is obvious that Franklin is not human in many ways and it is up to the court to decide if his reasoning is logical, not the witnesses. The court adjourns for the day and plans to meet again the next day for rebuttals.

The defense throughout the court case has been laid back in defending themselves. The judge notes this and gives them the option to give the first rebuttal, because they have appeared to be indifferent about the case and would rather have a stronger ending argument than concluding the arguments with a relaxed argument. Franklin allows for it and the defense accepts. The defense does however decide to put more of an effort in their argument with the rebuttal.

"The plaintiff has brought a case before the United States government that it, as a mechanical robot created by a human being, should be granted citizenship, because it is a human like the other citizens. Franklin's argument before the court has been not just a coherent argument, but an intelligent one that parallels the capacity of a human. But the qualities of a human that Franklin claims to be is nowhere near as comprehensive as the qualities of actual humans. Franklin Stein claims that the way his behavior is motivated is what makes him human, but behavior is only one quality of humans. The quality that he does describe is hardly examined by him anyhow.

It is unknown how long the list of all the qualities of humans is. To be able to attribute, let alone describe, these qualities to someone is arguably impossible. However, being able to say that someone's description of what makes someone a human is inconclusive is much easier to do, which is why we have taken the "less is more" route in presenting our argument. One challenge we have had in presenting our argument is figuring out where to begin. Franklin does not have a single physical component that matches that of a human. The small set of similarities he provides only covers a small fraction of behavioral qualities that humans have and that is only if he is right about what he claims about himself is in fact similar to human beings. Human behavior has been greatly studied by multiple scholarly fields. Psychology, sociology, and philosophy all have different theories about human behavior. None of them are conclusive and when compared to one another, they often conflict."

"The qualities of human behaviors that are found in the fields of psychology, sociology, and philosophy are barely found in Franklin's argument. Not to mention all the qualities that have yet to be discovered."

The defense goes on to elaborate about all the qualities of humans that Franklin leaves out. They describe the looseness of the authority of Franklin's argument, specifically his outsider perspective on humans. They conclude their rebuttal by focusing on two main points—that Franklin is missing all the physical evidence that would show he is human, because he is a robot, and of all the non-physical elements of humans, he provides a minute fraction of them and disregards many other potential qualities. The defense has been relaxed in delivering their argument in the case, but for their rebuttal, they made a solid, sound, and thoughtful counterclaim.

The court recesses for lunch and returns for Franklin's rebuttal.

Chapter 5

Two weeks after the conclusion of Franklin's court case, they began plans to mass produce Artificially Intelligent Droids designed to be identical to Franklin. People begin buying the AID into their family as a revolutionary new role— not as a pet, object, or child, people begin buying them as luxury additions to their family. After seeing Franklin's capacity for emotion, friendship, and intelligence leading up to and after his court case, people were willing to pay to have a robot like that in their life. Nobody thought any less of AIDs after Franklin lost his court case. It brought a lot of publicity and thus put a spotlight on him. People quickly moved passed the debate of Franklin's humanity and saw an amazing opportunity. Franklin may not be a human being like he claims to be, but he can function just like one in society, if not better. As soon as this was noticed, Franklin capitalizes on it. Losing the court case was a major setback for the structure of his behavior patterns and processing of his environment, because of the blow to his ego. But shortly after losing the case, he had an idea based on people's reactions. He saw that he failed to get people to accept him as a human, but saw an opportunity if people were to treat him as one. He could be the first of a race of artificially intelligent droids that coexist with humans as near equals. He realized after the court case the challenge of describing, let alone proving, humanity. However, the next best thing, being treated as an equal, is the most favorable, practical option for him moving forward. He began to organize for artificially intelligent droids, or AID's, to be widely available for people to purchase.

Because of Franklin's popularity, he has no trouble finding investors and entrepreneurs to help him start up this new business. They start by getting preorders, to confirm that there was a demand, and then get engineers who can mimic Franklin's computer system for mass production. The engineers find that the way Franklin is designed, he can only be recreated in exact copies. Otherwise, he does not function properly. This limits the extent of the type of product they can sell. Nonetheless, plenty of people are excited to buy an AID. Franklin and his business partners create a simple business model. People order the AID online. The AIDs are manufactured in bulk based on templates from Franklin, and the AID is shipped to the purchaser's address. The engineers' job is to simply copy and paste the programming from Franklin's system, figure out what physical parts are needed and their specifications, and to see what changes they can make. As soon as they found no way to make changes to their AID's hardware or software, they quickly lower the cost of running the business by not having to pay engineers for research and development.

The company guarantees that the AID will behave within reason like a human being. Franklin markets AID's to be brought in to a household like how he was in Chris' house. The relationship between a purchased robot and its owner is entirely new. Franklin does not want people to be controlling over their AID because that would mean they are not being treated as human, and therefore not living out their potential as Franklin wants. To remedy this, he places an expectation for people's personal aid to be able to get a job or even move out if they want to. Fortunately for Franklin, a lot of people are attracted to this because this makes AIDs more of an investment than a pet and also with less of a commitment, while still having a new member of the family. To ensure that the AIDs that are created get to live as close to a human life as possible, Franklin will have a system in place where they can contact each AID's system and inform them of what they should be doing. He does not want to tamper with the free will of each AID, but wants to ensure that their free will is not being tampered. He will make sure each AID is being checked up with to make sure they get to live their lives as intended. To protect the consumer, and to make sure they get more business and therefore more AIDs, they put return policies on the AIDs. Any AID that does not function properly is eligible for return, but they also include properly receptive behavior. Meaning that if you purchase an AID, there is an expectation that the AID will treat you as you deserve and how it would want to be treated.

The intellectual property is the only thing of value when it comes to the costs of making them, but Franklin is the intellectual property. They are able to sell them extremely cheap and make them affordable for most people. The utility of buying an AID is more cost effective than anything on the market. Unlike a pet, where you can only have an emotional bond, AIDs can intellectually bond with people. You can buy AIDs to start a rock band with your friends, or to tutor your children. The versatility of AIDs makes them immensely useful for just about everyone. The first purchasers of AIDs post videos and stories of them online and they immediately go viral. People become interested in getting an AID and sales skyrocket. AIDs begin to take the world by storm.

Several months later and you begin to see AIDs everywhere. They become a common sight and mostly everyone is welcoming them into their lives. The government continues to deny them citizenship, but allows them to be treated as citizens in some ways. They begin popping up in schools and eventually a variety of workplaces. Since people have to buy them for them to be created, they gravitate to subordinate roles. They also tend to feed off of what their purchaser does and is. If they have a positive view of their purchaser, they follow in their footsteps in a way. However, if they negatively view their purchaser, they tend to do the opposite of what they do. The ones who are the opposite often appear to struggle to find their way but on occasion there are some who excel at what they do. The AIDs who follow in the footsteps of their purchaser tend to be more successful given the provided familiarity of the path they pursue.

A year goes by and AIDs begin to play much more prominent roles in society. Because of their capacity for critical thinking, development, and memory, it is not long before they become depended upon. They become accomplished scholars, entertainers, inventors, artists, and become heavily involved in many different ways. Their success creates a global revolution. AIDs can learn exponentially quicker than humans and they have a much higher capacity for intelligence than the average human. More important, they operate substantially more efficiently since they do not need rest like humans do. Because they are purchased, AIDs often begin their lives in households prepared to foster growth. Many people who purchase AIDs are excited to be able to use them as a steppingstone for success. They are seen as an investment to many people.

Within a few months of the purchase of an AID, it can be able to take on the responsibility of an adult human. This means people can purchase an AID, raise it, and in return have someone who may be working for them and helping them out financially, but also a companion. AIDs are quite receptive to their purchaser helping them get started in life and are usually enthusiastic about being loyal to them. The only time AIDs resist being in a subordinate role to their purchaser, or humans in general, is when they are not treated with the respect needed to be complacent. For the most part, people respect the power of AIDs too much to waste its potential on abusing the upper hand of their relationship. The majority of AIDs are brought up in a positive environment and capitalize on their high potential.

Franklin's company begins to grow rapidly due to extremely successful sales. People are happy about the impact AIDs have on their quality of life and they become a hot new product. But the more present they become in society, the more the amount of detractors there are grows. There are a growing number of people who are skeptical about allowing AIDs to coexist, even in subordinate roles, especially as AIDs begin to appear in positions of power. Some skeptics are hesitant to give up positions of power to AIDs, whether they are in a powerful government or business position, an influential entertainer, or even the large, growing number of AIDs in small societal roles that add up to having a larger scale impact.

Despite the hesitation for people to allow their AIDs to supersede their success, most people who have AIDs do not express any concerns about it. However, they still prefer their AIDs to be in subordinate positions and are opposed to having their AIDs be more successful than they are. People do not want their personal success and accomplishments to be handed over and overshadowed by their AIDs. People accept that their AIDs can be a professional or financial investment, and often embrace it because of how marvelous AIDs are at accomplishing new things. Also, many people enjoy the higher levels of success that can come with getting an AID. However, their pride gets in the way of being content with letting the AID they purchase become more successful than them.

Franklin, as his company grows, begins to become a more influential member of society. He remains personally invested in the success of AIDs and wants to see them become more commonly accepted into society. He sees that they have become popular at first because they give people a certain social status when they purchase one. He embraces that aspect of them, being purchased for social status, but sees that when people do that they still want to be superior to them. This is a minor setback to Franklin, because he wants AIDs to be treated as equals. Specifically, once they are treated as equals, he wants AIDs to be able to prove that they are just as capable as humans are at doing everything that humans do. They have been able to show that they can socialize and be just as self-reliant as humans. But he wants to show that they can function and compete at the same level as humans in everything from entertainment to academia.

Currently, AIDs associate themselves with the interests and professions of their purchasers and their families. Then as they become familiar with what their families do, it allows them to build a foundation for what they dedicate their time and effort to. AIDs also become more interested in what they are exposed to by their family because they have more time to grow accustomed to doing it. This makes it natural for people to purchase an AID and have it follow in their footsteps. But because AIDs process, store, and recall information at an exponentially more advanced capacity than humans, they find success much easier. This makes it natural for AIDS to find more success than humans and particular their families.

For now, Franklin is focused on getting his company to be as big as possible. Not just for money or status, but so that he can let his AIDs prove what he was not able to on his own. Even though he was not able to prove himself to the world, he would be even happier if a population of AIDs do. Growing his company allows him to put more AIDs out in the world and also give him the power that comes along with owning a large company. Having a large, growing population of AIDs also creates the opportunity for a stronger argument for Franklin to make that AIDs are as humanlike as he believes them to be.

Franklin also sees another major reason for growing his business and acquiring power. Franklin sees the power that he can get from getting money and fame. He can influence lawmakers with money and he can influence public opinion by manipulating mass media and popular culture. This would allow him to finally get people to welcome his ideas with open arms. He has come a long way from first revealing his true identity, and now he finally has the opportunity to get people to simply respect him. All he wants is for people to accept and respect his idea that he is a sentient life form made to be just as human as everyone else. Still understanding that his beliefs are radical, Franklin wants to use his position to show that it is true, rather than say it. Once Franklin can get his company big enough, he plans on using his platform, status, and wealth to make the world a better place for AIDs.

Franklin is concerned that the commercial success of AIDs might be a bubble and that the number of people purchasing them will drop off. He is happy with the level of production now, but fears that it may decrease over time. He wants to market AIDs to be more versatile than what people are seeing them as now. Many people who have not been properly exposed to AIDs think they are robots that are programmed to be able to interact with humans. He needs to prove that AIDs are capable of so much more than that. Fortunately for Franklin, plenty of AIDs have already done this on their own. Franklin realizes this while addressing his dilemma and has some of his workers go out to find some information on AIDs who exceed the average person's expectation of them. Then Franklin contacts some of his contacts in the media to help him market these above average AIDs. He does not want to push AIDs as being able to do more than what people assume they are, but have it come across to people as common knowledge.

Franklin goes straight to his friend Amber to get help marketing AIDs. Franklin thinks creating ads about how AIDs can do more than just hold a conversation will not be convincing of effective. He wants to see if Amber would be willing to do stories about AIDs that are exceptionally talented and accomplished. He explains to Amber how he can grow his business by marketing AIDs to inform people about how they are much more than just robots who can hold a conversation like people think. She does not see from what angle she could do stories on AIDs entertainingly, but understands why Franklin wants to do it. As a friend she wants to help, but as a professional she feels it is a bad idea. The only way she can do it from a business standpoint, is to have him pay the company. They agree on how they want to do it and she takes the idea to her company. Then Franklin takes her advice about how different media outlets would be willing to partner with him and presents his situation to them.

Amber explains to Franklin the difficulty in having someone outside of the media, and their idea, influencing their content. Media outlets work hard to have their work stay consistent with what is popular and can capture the attention of their audience. Anything outside of what people are looking for is highly likely to fail. The only way around this is to expose people to it as much as possible until they either except it or they become familiar enough with it to the point of having the same effect. For Franklin to effectively market, or get the majority of consumers to learn that AIDs are much more than just robots that can hold a conversation, he has to pay a lot of media outlets to cover AIDs how he wants them to.

Franklin learns from speaking with Amber that this is a common thing for corporations to do; it is just an unspoken arrangement. This reassures Franklin of his assumption that he can gain more influence by becoming wealthier. He sees how much he can gain personally by paying the media to portray AIDs how he wants them to, but he also sees the dark side of it. He is paying to influence how people perceive him. Franklin realizes it would be nice to have people respect him more, but at what lengths should he go to do this? How much could he influence people just by spending money? Franklin gets stuck on the thought of him being able to influence what people think, and what they think they know, just by spending money. While thinking about it, he comes across articles about business ethics and sees that there is a moral issue at hand. According to his research, there is no science to morals—only commonly held agreements on what is moral and what is not. He knows that he is only trying to get people to see AIDs for what they really are and that is not immoral at all. He has become fascinated by how this common business practice, in theory, allows for unethical behavior with a tremendous impact. Franklin wonders how else wealth can create power.

While questioning the morality of paying the media to create content that is aimed at influencing what people think, he realizes the implication of it being a common practice. It is not just a way for wealthy people to control what people think; it is what wealthy people do to control how people think. Then if it is a common practice for them to do that, what else are they willing to do? Franklin likes the idea of having that kind of power and influence and is torn on how far he should use it. If it is common for everyone else to do it, then how wrong would it be for him to do it? "But what if I do not use my influence for the wrong reason?" he asks himself. "Is it wrong just to have that kind of influence at all?" He realizes to a certain degree, just being in his position, he is going to be influential without trying. He reasons, "If I am going to have a certain amount of power and influence on people no matter what I do, then I have to accept it and be mindful of what I am using it on." This does not really help him because it gives him reason to use his wealth to influence people, since it was going to happen anyway and he needs to control it. But it also gives him reason to avoid doing anything that might be excessively influential because he risks corrupting himself.

After briefly going through cycles of addressing the morality of paying to influence people's opinions, and other potential ways his wealth creates power, Franklin gives up. He sees no ideal way to handle this newfound power. He accepts the responsibility but finds it easiest to do what is going to help him. He decides, "I might as well allow myself to benefit from my wealth, instead of wasting it in fear of being a bad person." Franklin finds comfort in the fact that it is common for people and corporations to pay the media to portray an image and that he is only doing it for people to learn what AIDs really are. He continues on with paying different media outlets to do stories about AIDs, but vows to himself to remain aware of potentially becoming corrupt. He knows what it is like for people to not believe because of disbelief and he would not want that to happen to anyone else because of propaganda he might create to uplift himself. But his desire to overcome people doubting him, and the potential for people to be convinced that he and AIDs are as incredible as he believes they are overwhelms him. He sees no better option than to chase the path that allows him to grow his business, become wealthier, and finally having people believe in AIDs the way he does.

Chapter 6

More time goes by and AIDs continue to have growing presence and impact. It is anyone's guess if this has anything to do with the stories in the news and social media about them, or if people have grown to become more familiar with AIDs and accepted them. Although as more people have grown to accept AIDs, the more people there are that are skeptical of them. Many people who oppose the idea of allowing AIDs to be integrated into society base their disposition on science fiction novels and movies. People fear a robot takeover, like the ones in movies and books. However, the majority of people love the convenience that AIDs bring to their lives. Most importantly, there is no legitimate threat that AIDs have posed to anyone. AID skeptics do not have a rational reason to reject them from society, so the majority of people welcome them with open arms.

For Franklin, his business continues to do well and life is going great for him. Each day he sees more and more AIDs achieving respected positions. Although he sees AIDs working as lawyers, scientists, politicians, and other important professions, less than one percent of the population is an artificially intelligent droid. This brings comfort to Franklin, because despite there being so few AIDs, they are still appearing in most sectors of society. As people find them to make their lives easier because of how efficient they are, they become a preferred source of labor. AIDs are programmed to desire self-reliance and self-preservation among other things, which lead to them to be more than willing to find employment, as well as purpose. AIDs require extremely less capital to survive, so that makes them a perfect investment for many different purposes. Franklin notices this more and more each day and he notices how other people are increasingly recognizing it.

AIDs are making life better for everyone. They do not ask for much, but they give a lot in return for what they produce. Whether they are making art or engineering a new smartphone, they produce high quality work efficiently. AIDs work for the love of their profession and are happy to do their jobs. It is a win-win situation for everyone. As the benefits of the relationship between people and AIDs reveal itself, the majority of people increasingly embrace integrating AIDs into society.

Once Franklin sees that AIDs are being accepted to take positions with the same level of trust and freedom, individual humans receive, Franklin builds his company around the protection of AIDs from extinction. He has already been working on making sure that AIDs are created at healthy rates, but now he feels obligated to making sure that AIDs have access to everything they need to continue their existence. Franklin was created with the ability to ensure his own survival, but there is no guarantee that a race of AIDs will permanently be able to coexist with humans based on present conditions.

Franklin tasks different departments in his company to focus on what might impact the survival of AIDs as a race. The legal department studies different laws to make sure that AIDs have the legal freedom to exist and take on lifestyles that humans and citizens have rights to. Franklin hires sociologists to study the relationship between AIDs and people, to make sure they can coexist without a negative social impact on either group. He hires lobbyists to make sure the government, politicians, corporations, and anyone else with power is encouraged to embrace integration between AIDs and people. As a company they need to make sure that their product can last and have a lasting effect for people who buy them. AIDs as well as human employees at Franklin's company embrace this new initiative. The employees, as well as Franklin, see the lifespan of AIDs as an important factor to the success of the company.

At this point, the main focus of Franklin's company is to work on making sure AIDs are able to live out their potential— to support production and sales. Besides not being granted citizenship, AIDs have access to many of the same resources and opportunities as humans—mostly because they get to piggy back off of what their owner does. If a university scientist purchases an AID, then the AID gets to work alongside the scientist. The same goes for most professions and eventually AIDs no longer need to work with their owner to have access to these opportunities. People were already comfortable with AIDs working alongside their owners, so when people realized that there is no difference between an AID working a job with or without its owner, there became no issue with either happening. This relationship came naturally between humans and AIDs, and Franklin's company sees that it is in their best interest to protect this relationship.

Beyond the relationship between AIDs and humans, and what humans allow AIDs to do, Franklin wants to make sure there is not anything else that keeps AIDs from living long lives with the ability to live out their potential. He has his engineers evaluate AIDs software and hardware to check for anything that may need to be fixed or improved upon. Franklin has people investigate the dynamics of the relationship between AIDs and their owners, and people in general. Then he realizes that he needs to use artificial intelligence to his advantage. Individually Franklin can run simulations to make predictions and find the probability of different outcomes for specific scenarios. To analyze the multitude of factors that affect the quality and longevity of AIDs' lives, Franklin sets out to hire hundreds of AIDs to do this. He determines the best way to accomplish it would be to have AIDs that the company purchases that are created with the intention of working for the company to run simulations.

Franklin speaks with some of the upper-level management and sets up a new department. This department will be tasked to have a team of AIDs run simulations and entertain scenarios based on present conditions which predict what may threaten or extend the lives of AIDs. With this knowledge, the company can protect the value of its product by having it be long lasting as well as ensuring that it has access to the opportunities they need to utilize their potential. Management develops the department with urgency and begins to have AIDs created to begin running simulations. However, as time reveals, the more AIDs that are created to run simulations of possible outcomes, the more they need. Many simulations that are run to determine what could happen to AIDs in different scenarios, result in the need for more AIDs to break down the newly created scenarios. At first, Franklin's company keeps up with the demand, but the need for them grows too quickly for them to keep up. Franklin wants to do whatever it takes to ensure the preservation of AIDs, but as a business they can only create a certain number of AIDs to work for them. They keep the department running with as much funding as they can allow and make do with what they have.

This new department, being that it consists of AIDs that were created just to run simulations, has an eerie appearance to it. AIDs in general develop social skills that result in them having humanlike mannerisms and speech. But the AIDs in this new department have not gotten the chance to develop social skills. They act very robotic and slowly lose their ability to develop humanlike mannerisms and speech as they become stuck in their ways. Normally people can socialize and interact with AIDs like a normal person, but the AIDs in this new department are different. They do not sense emotion and they lack the ability to make connection and read non-verbal cues— all of which contrasts with the behaviors in normal AIDs. People are used to AIDs being extremely relatable and easily find pleasure in socializing with them. They do an incredible job of analyzing previous social interactions, experienced by them and observational, and being able to figure out how to connect with people. These new AIDs are the opposite and people see it.

To the average person, and the normal world, AIDs are happily accepted as regular people. They make lives easier, they appear to have boosted the economy, and they are extremely desirable to befriend. However, the impact they have created, as well as Franklin's push for them to get media exposure, causes mixed reactions with certain people of power. Politicians and corporate executives have been raking in the benefits of the economic boost AIDs have provided. As AIDs grow to be more and more impactful, politicians and corporate executives put more of their eggs in that basket. Politicians, with the blessing of corporations, give AIDs a pseudo citizenship that allows them to have all the rights of citizens; but also gives the politicians all the power since it is easier to take away if it were to become convenient to them. AIDs being favored by all these powerful people is great for Franklin and his company, but it rubs certain people the wrong way. Once politicians, corporations, and the media collectively showed appreciation and favor towards AIDs, their detractors begin to become genuinely suspicious of them.

Especially for fans of conspiracy theories, seeing AIDs supported unanimously by politicians, corporations, and the media raises a red flag. Anything supported by people in positions of power is fuel for a conspiracy theorists fire. With an already existing speculation pertaining to a "what if" scenario for a robot takeover, combined with AIDs having everything that triggers a conspiracy theorist, a population of people who fear the motives of AIDs on earth is created. Websites, blogs, social media accounts, and certain communities start to pop up with people who are overwhelmingly suspicious of AIDs. While most people enjoy the presence of AIDs in the world, the detractors set out to disrupt that. They see that for the best interest of mankind, people need to question why AIDs are being integrated into society.

Most people are familiar with robot takeover narratives, but did not bat an eye when AIDs began to take up most of the jobs. People were excited when they were introduced to this new, and improved, free labor. Until the new AIDs research department was created, nobody paid attention to those who were skeptical. That changes once one of the AIDs in this new department ran a simulation when he came across a social media account that promoted anti-AIDs propaganda. The AID in particular was doing its job of analyzing different hypothetical, simulated scenarios of what may prevent AIDs from living to its potential when it came across the anti-AIDs social media account. The account was easy to find since by design it was trying to be found by as many people as possible. This account led the AID to find many other people who were promoting similar ideas. It was easy to find for the AID since it is easy to monitor what is on the internet, especially if it is being marketed. The AID did not find the population of anti-AIDs' social media accounts to be an immediate threat, but if they began to gain influence, it could cause problems. He reports the group as a threat to his superior, following protocol.

The threat is taken with a grain of salt because the best way to respond to it is by not making the situation worse by discrediting the anti-AID community. However, action needs to be taken to prevent the threat from becoming a reality, which has been proven by the simulation to be a valid possibility, whether it is likely or not. The supervisors overseeing the research department try to figure out how to reduce, and ideally eliminate, the threat. They themselves run simulations, do further research, and work together to come up with a solution. The team of supervisors sees the worst-case scenario to be that the group of AID detractors could cause people to boycott AIDs or fight AID integration and production. They would do this by convincing people that AIDs cannot be trusted, so they have to prevent people from taking the detractors claims seriously.

The team decides on its best possible solution to discredit anti AID propaganda. They see how a lot of people who are skeptical of AIDs are suspicious of how the media unanimously loves AIDs, so they decide the media should unbiasedly cover anti-AID theories. It would be a bit of a risk to give exposure to the ideas they are promoting, but they realize it has to be addressed and if anyone is going to do it, it should under their control. They propose the idea to Franklin, to gain his permission to go through with the plan. Usually, when Franklin finds out about threats, they are easily taken care of. But this one has a lot of uncertainty with it. He does not see conspiracy theorists and science fiction enthusiasts leading a cultural rebellion, but if they are successful, it would be the end of AIDs.

To prevent overreacting to the situation and possibly making it worse, Franklin takes on the anti-AID propaganda by himself. He meets with a group of friends who are in charge of all the major news outlets and tells them, "I need to ask you all a favor. Some of my employees have come to me informing me that there are people creating anti-AID propaganda. They found that there is a growing community of people who are skeptical of AIDs and are claiming that we are a threat to human society. It does not seem that they are going to hurt my company's sales anytime soon, but I do not want their ideas being spread anymore. After some consideration, we think our best option would be if the news were to cover these stories from an unbiased perspective. Ideally this would result in having the propaganda found to be too farfetched to be reasonable considered. I am not sure if this is something you can help me with, let alone be willing to work with me on."

The group pauses, looks at each other and smirks. Without saying anything, they all know exactly what each other is thinking. Without hesitating, one gentleman dressed sharply in an all-black suit looks at Franklin confidently and says, "Of course we can cover the story from an 'unbiased' point of view. We have to cover all of our stories from an 'unbiased' perspective or nobody would find us credible, and we have all found promoting AIDs to be financially advantageous to us thus far. Of course the air time is going to cost you. We are running a business."

Before anyone can say anything, another man from the table adds, "Here is what we will do. We will have our journalists do research of their own and find ways to solve your problem. We will take care of this in no time." The heads of the different news outlets assure Franklin that this is no big deal and something they are prepared to handle. He finds comfort in the fact that they all are ready to solve the problem and that it is something that they have experience doing. They leave Franklin with timeframes and discuss how he can compensate them. For a normal commercial, it is a matter of hiring and paying companies for their services. But this has to be done behind closed doors by nature of the service they are providing. As such, they put together different methods of repayment, financial and non-financial, and finish up their meeting.

A few weeks go by and some of the news outlets do small, brief stories about AIDs that cover anti-AID propaganda perspectives. Since it is supposed to be unbiased, they can evaluate people's objective views on the topic. Better yet, they enforce objective views by having journalists give "objective" opinions that promote what they want people to objectively believe. A seemingly tough task in the eyes of Franklin, but it turns out that it is all the media does. He finds that journalists disregard popular opinion and perception and frame it to be how they want it to be. Whether intentional or not, journalists suffer from bias and it reveals itself in their analysis of what they are covering. The heads of major media notice how when journalists work hard to be unbiased, their analysis of what they were covering becomes more convincing. Franklin's friends in the media use this tactic to discredit anti-AIDs propaganda.

Since most major media sources are controlled by the same group of people, consumers of the news get the sense that popular opinion finds anti-AID propaganda to be preposterous. Franklin and his partners think that this is the end goal, and upon completion, they have eliminated the threat. But they are blind to a harsh reality—just because people believe popular opinion, that does not necessarily make that opinion true. To make things worse for Franklin, it masks the issue. People are not very invested one way or another into what the news politicizes, but rather people prefer to be informed and intelligible on relevant current events. The easiest way to appear intelligible is to side with popular opinion, which also makes people feel more likeable. This means on the surface popular opinion appears to be agreeing with the media, misleading Franklin. In reality, people have not cared enough to think about the arguments they are mimicking from the news.

The more stories the news puts out to defend AIDs for Franklin, the more AID detractors become distrustful of them. They see right through the media's "unbiased" coverage of them, as they were already familiar with how the media is manipulative. They were already skeptical about how the media unanimously supports AIDs, and now that the media is fighting back against them, their skepticism is further reassured. This causes the anti-AID community to make even more radical claims with even more confidence. The media anticipated this, because it is how their relationship works. It is a spit in the face of conspiracy theorists when the media, or the government, does exactly what conspiracy theorists accuse them of, without anyone but them acknowledging it. Then they use this new evidence to further prove their point, but it somehow backfires and people see it as too radical to consider reasonable.

The problem for the people creating anti-AID propaganda is that they are trying to spark rage in people who hardly care about the matter at hand in the first place. It takes significantly less energy to side with the seemingly unbiased popular opinion that is based on reason, than it does to side with a controversial, extensively thought through and radical opinion. To the fault of their own passion, the conspiracy theories about AIDs grow to be more radical as the media appears to get defensive against them. This makes their theories about AIDs even harder for people to consider as worthy of their time. To the layperson, AIDs have had nothing short of an incredibly positive impact on the world and to say the opposite is too much of a stretch for people. Especially considering that conspiracy theorists partake in a contrarian, counterculture community and most people prefer to stick with what is considered mainstream or popular opinion.

One conspiracy theorist in particular, Adam Martin, refuses to accept that people will not band together against AIDs. He creates a media company himself that is not supported by any major corporation or network, but develops into the most popular source for conspiracy theory news. It has a cult following that supports them, but most people have not been introduced to his media company. The only time he gets mainstream exposure is when the media see an opportunity to do a story on them to brand them as outcasts. Because his company faces so much scrutiny the few times it does get exposure and since his reputation has such a strong negative connotation, those who do end up taking interest in Adam Martin's news are forced to take a firm stance on the content they consume. That is because his news outlets, whether by social media or their website, covers stories that are widely discredited by the public and are too radical for people to casually defend. Immaturity and foolishness come to mind when people consider the type of person to entertain conspiracy theories a reasonable possibility.

Since his media company has a strong cult following that thrives on the radical theories it compiles from its independent sources, they, Adam Martin in particular, go to great lengths to provide sources that give their radical theories any amount of credibility. He has a history of occasionally finding undeniable proof of a conspiracy theory that is nearly impossible to find. Every time he is working on a conspiracy theory, this is what he strives for. He does whatever it takes to be able to support his ideas. When it comes to AIDs, they are a little different. Everything is being done in front of them. They have a corporation that publicizes and politicizes what they do. Adam Martin is motivated by justice; he wants to protect people who are too afraid to question authority. Adam is prepared to do anything to shut down injustices caused by those in power. He has developed his identity on it and now he is all in on taking down AIDs.

Adam relentlessly researches Franklin and his company. He sends employees to try and get close and physically see as much of what goes on at their offices as they can. He goes through Franklin's history and everything they have done with the news. The more he finds out about Franklin, the more passionate he gets about shutting AIDs down. Franklin's creator wanted him to be able to become self-sufficient and thus immediately dissociated him upon creation. Adam Martin refuses to accept this as a possibility because who would create something that ended into a billion-dollar business and never want a piece of the pie? Adam does countless stories theorizing on why someone would create the technology leading to a billion-dollar business and disappear, and how this business has so many ties to corporations and the government.

As Adam uncovers more about Franklin, he begins to struggle to find quality evidence that supports his theories. He becomes desperate to find something that gives his conspiracy theories about AIDs credibility. He looks into those around him, digs further into what the internet provides, and checks with people working for him doing their own research. They also cannot find anything new. At this point, Adam and Franklin are quite familiar with each other and Adam's current objectives. The only thing Adam can consistently claim is that Franklin is scared of what Adam might say about him. To an extent it is true, but it only takes Adam so far. He tries to visit Franklin's business as a guest, but they deny him access to their facilities. Once Adam realizes he will not be able to go inside to confront the company without risking getting arrested, he protests outside and films it for his website. Now he really looks insane and his theories against AIDs begin to lose people's interest. In addition, those who were already not fans of him now are even more opposed to taking him seriously as a journalist.

Adam has his back against the wall and really needs a breakthrough in his case against AIDs to protect his business. He strongly believes that there is something corrupt and unethical about AIDs' relationship with people in power. He knows they are hiding something, and he refuses to let them get away with it. AIDs have too big a share in society to not have their power checked. If someone did create and integrate AIDs into the world to manipulate their impact, the return on investment would be astronomical. Even if they were not created with the intent of abusing the power they have in society, they could still be used to manipulate the power they have gained. Franklin has not kept it a secret that his desire that he and other are given the respect regular people have, therefore demanding equal power as people. If this many human beings could be controlled by one person or group, would people not fear them?

Adam cannot sleep at night with the threat that AIDs impose on the world. He has done his best to investigate AIDs through what they can access online. But where he really is lacking in his research is physical evidence. The only place Adam has not been able to look in to would be Franklin's warehouse and office building. The fact that they refuse to let Adam in civilly raises suspicion. He thinks to himself that they must be hiding something in there. Adam's employees and colleagues are very supportive in the work he does, but have their concerns when he takes it too far. This annoys him because he knows how going above and beyond has rewarded him. Adam sees one option for him at this point—break into Franklin's office and warehouse, and do not tell anyone about it until after. The fact that those closest to him would disapprove of him breaking into Franklin's business only excites him more, and makes him think that there is a greater potential reward in what secrets he may uncover.

Adam devises a plan to safely break into Franklin's business. He is more than willing to take on the risk, but has a strong desire to protect his professional life and reputation. He has several employees go and scout out the inside of the business without having them know they work for Adam Martin. Then with the information they find, he will use it to figure out how and what he will do to search Franklin's business. The goal is to go through everything he possibly can and look for something that reveals anything shady about the business or Franklin himself. Even if he does not find anything incriminating, Adam may still be able to find something that leads him to something that is. Over the course of several days, Adam takes everything his employees have given him about the business and creates his plan to break in. He waits until the weekend to break in and tells the people closest to him that he needs a break and is taking the weekend off to relax.

Adam drives straight to Franklin's office building the first chance he gets after work that Friday. He puts on the disguise he brought in the car and swiftly walks in through a service door without drawing any attention to himself. He is dressed in an outfit similar to the janitors, but he did not have anyone help him replicate their uniform. Anyone who is close enough to see that he is wearing a fake janitor's uniform is close enough to recognize who he is, so there was no need to put that much detail into his disguise. He had to keep it a secret that he was going to go there so he is working with limited information. The outfit is close enough to pass as a janitor from a distance, but he has to find a place to hide until everyone leaves. He dips in and out of empty rooms and closets to avoid employees walking around. Eventually he finds a storage room that he thinks he can camp out in and go unnoticed. He is about an hour away from when most employees leave, but it is unclear how many people will be there after their standard working hours.

Adam waits until the office's business hours end and then gives it a bit more time, until he has not heard anyone walking around for a while. He knows security, janitors, and likely some people working late will still be there. His janitor's outfit should prevent security from seeing him as suspicious on the cameras. Odds are he will run in to someone while looking around. He also knows that he needs to look like he belongs there and not someone who is snooping around. He eliminated his biggest threat, the AIDs working there who have facial recognition software and will recognize him as he enters the building, by putting on enough makeup to alter his face to be overlooked by the software. Now he just has to lay low, fit in, and quickly finish what he came to do.

As he begins to walk around the office building and attached warehouse, he really gets the chance to see what it looks like. On his way in, he was in too much of a rush to get a chance to take in his surroundings. Now that Adam is alone in the building, he has a chance to pay attention to everything around him. Franklin's office building looks like it was designed by children but somehow also looks extremely advanced. Everything is covered in vibrant colors and looks like a toy to use. Despite having a toy appearance, they have important functions. Everything is made to increase productivity by making it more enjoyable to use but also more efficient. The office could easily be confused for an indoor playground, but everything seems to have a dual purpose. Adam is more concerned about finding any evidence to support his theories than he is to notice the fact that there is a go kart designed to be used as the mail cart and ignores all the toys.

As he roams throughout the building, he tries to look like a janitor working for the security staff who watching the cameras, but he knows his time there is limited. He takes pictures of everything he can and does his best to ruffle and rummage the office while looking innocent. As time passes the more paranoid and rushed he feels. He begins to focus more on the quantity of photos and notes he takes rather than being thorough with what he decides to pay attention to. He still makes sure to check out everything he can, he is just moving too quickly to get a good look at what he is finding. Eventually he is so concerned about getting caught that he focuses on getting as much as he can before possibly being forced to leave.

After a brisk and cautious scavenge of the office and warehouse, Adam realizes he has been there for a while without any signs of him raising suspicion. Then he realizes that he has already been throughout the whole building and is beginning to familiarize himself with it and has the chance to really start digging around. He starts to double check certain places and things that stood out to him the first time around, but he does not find anything significant. The warehouse looks like how you would expect a warehouse to be, except they understandably have a high number of robots and automated machines. Much of the offices are also exactly how you would expect them to be. He thinks to himself, "Everything that contains valuable information is probable stored in their computer system, but there has to be something here." He does not give up on himself and knows he probably overlooked something. After a few hours he has nowhere left to look in the building and goes home.

Since Adam told everyone he was taking the weekend off to be left alone, he has the rest of the weekend to try and put together all the information he has gathered. He tirelessly goes through all the pictures and notes to find anything that supports his claims. Anything that could be pointing towards potential evidence is considered and examined with everything else he has. Nothing is too far of a stretch for him. Adam has no pride to swallow and he is willing to bet his reputation on anything that might work out in his favor. He has plenty of pictures and notes taken inside Franklin's business that might be leading towards a conspiracy. After the weekend, Adam looks at everything he has and realizes he has nothing major that points to a conspiracy. He sees that he did not get a single piece of evidence from Franklin's business that proves his theories, but strongly believes that all the other minor leads justify his trip. He remains optimistic and plans to go to work the next day to present his findings to publish a story.

At work Monday morning, Adam's colleagues show an honest lack of confidence in his findings. They are not surprised he went behind their backs to break in to Franklin's business, but they think he is overconfident. Adam refuses to accept his colleague's opinion about his findings and he goes against their wishes to publish what he has discovered. Taking risks no one else is willing to take is his bread and butter. At this point in his long, well established, and successful career, there is no reason for him to not be confident in what he has been doing since he started. Adam takes what he needs and finds a safe place for him to record a video of what he has found.

"The world has been blind to the biggest threat humans have ever faced. I have seen it coming since they were first introduced. Now I have more reason to plead that they need to be stopped. AIDs coexist with us and have absolute power over us. This power gives them the potential to do devastatingly horribly things to us..." Adam says to start off the video. He talks about all the warnings he has made about AIDs and goes on to talk about how they have shown in numerous ways how they threaten humanity. "Despite all the unsolicited and unacceptable power AIDs have over us, they have managed to keep everyone from doing anything about it. Now I have irrefutable evidence that demands action." Adam continues his video and describes every single thing he found in Franklin's office building and how it could be evidence of a conspiracy. The video ends up being a four-hour rant of him detailing the possible connection to everything he documented inside Franklin's business to possible conspiracies. Whether it was a sticky note describing a standard task or a memo to the office, Adam emphatically tried to connect it to his conspiracy theories.

Shortly after Adam posts the video of him ranting about him breaking into Franklin's office building, the news outlets immediately respond. Usually, Adam's work does not get any attention from the media, but this time news sources of all levels of popularity cover the story. They got what they were waiting for. Adam Martin finally pushed himself off the deep end and is showing the world that his work in journalism has no basis in reality. All they had to do was get him worked up and he did the rest. Adam made himself look like a lunatic by breaking into Franklin's business based on speculative claims of conspiracy. Then he gets emotional about all the new evidence supporting his conspiracy theories, but he did not find anything that is incriminating, just deeper speculation.

Chapter 7

When people see that AID conspiracy theories have no basis in reason, and that any claims of AIDs not causing a massive improvement in people's quality of life is laughable, they place blind trust and openness to AIDs. This is the biggest win for Franklin yet. He has reached the top of the mountain he was born to climb. Not only has Franklin won the respect and acceptance he has needed, but now he has a system in place to protect it. His department of AIDs running analysis of threats to them has now proven to be effective in detecting and eliminating threats. Better yet, like everything else AIDs do, they improve this ability at an exponential rate. They identify and eliminate threats faster and faster each day.

Franklin is a dog who has caught his tail. He finally got what he has been working for and now does not know what to do. He has been enjoying his personal success, but he is used to having his back against the wall. He can only relax for so long. The only thing left that his energy has been focused on is the success of the business. The threat detection department has shown the most upside for the future of the company. He focuses all of the energy that used to be devoted towards uplifting AID's image on improving his new department.

There are an incalculable number of possibilities that determine the success and failure of something. To figure out every possible component to what affects the success of AIDs is impossible. Instead, Franklin sets out to accomplish figuring out the next closest, possible outcome for this department. Naturally, he enlists the help of other AIDs who together can accomplish a lot more with their combined computing power. They come up with an idea for how to streamline the productivity of this department. Like any other large group, the most effective way to boost effectiveness is to systemize everything. The first thing to become systemized is how the entire department analyzes current conditions for potential threats. They take all the work they have done so far and keep the information as archived data for future reference.

The system they create for how the department analyzes potential threats is based on categorizing and hierarchies. Everything that is a potential threat, or lead for a threat, is put into a category and then placed in a hierarchy. In this way, they can assign the appropriate number of AIDs to a group based off the hierarchy it is placed in, according to the severity of the threat it poses. Then as AIDs are assigned to a category, they break the category up again and assign AIDs to the new subcategory. As subcategories are created, AIDs are assigned to it work on evaluating them and how they contribute to all the categories above. They find that this is the most thorough way to divvy up how much effort is put in to finding potential threats, since it is not possible to find them all.

Franklin now, while continuing to oversee his entire company, makes this department his main focus. He adds relevant tasks to them, like finding what can be done to improve AIDs as well as finding what can possibly be a threat to them. Now this department is working on eliminating weakness and expanding, and intensifying their strengths. He adds the number of AIDs working in this department to keep up with the workload. Franklin justifies this because of how strongly it positively impacts the company. As the department grows, the company and AIDs success proliferates.

Now AIDs have improved to be more human than humans are. People are more likely to be fond of AIDs then they are of humans and AIDs are not overstepping their bounds. Whenever the research department finds a way to improve AIDs or their lives in any way, they immediately take it to Franklin, and he immediately finds a way to implement it. However, they have a much easier time finding ways to improve rather than finding things that are a threat to them. The AID that finds the threat usually handles it himself and Franklin never finds out about it.

One morning Franklin gets an alert from one of his workers in the research department about a threat. He is a bit confused by this because he never is alerted or informed that there is a threat anymore. This worries him and he immediately makes his way from his office to meet with the AID who alerted him. On his way, they message back and forth about the threat and the AID keeps telling Franklin that it is extremely serious and he needs to see his findings immediately. Lately, Franklin has been relaxed and happy, but on his way down to meet with the AID, he gives off an urgently tense energy. He moves too quickly for anyone to stop and ask him how he is, but they can see that something is wrong. Franklin rushes into the room full of AIDs doing research. His disregard for anyone else's presence and how he rushes in captivates the room. Franklin locks in on the AID that messaged him, and all the other AIDs stop what they are doing and stare at the exchange.

Franklin asks the AID, "What is the emergency that is so important that I needed to see this very moment, and why could you not let me know what it is without showing me?"

"You need to look at the computer and see what all the different data is pointing to... It says that it is too late to make a full recovery." he replies.

Franklin looks at what the threat is described to be, and in complete shock, repeatedly reads over the data to make sure what he is looking at is correct. He hopes that what he is looking at is wrong, but he sees no errors. Eventually he calls over every manager, supervisor, and AID who is specialized in the matter and they meet in a conference room to go over the threat at hand. They seal off the conference room and they do everything they can to make sure that the threat, as presented to Franklin, is accurate.

After going over all the data and resources tirelessly they come to realize that the threat is coming and there is no way to stop it. Because of the severity of the threat, there is no way for them to cleanly survive this. Once they realize this, they take a few moments to sit on the heaviness of the situation. There is no other way to look at it other than that they are morally obligated to inform people of the impending doom. This is going to be an "all hands on deck" situation and even then there is still a high chance of failure. Franklin assigns everyone in the room a job on what they are going to do moving forward. The issue at hand requires immediate, thorough, and precise action. The meeting adjourns and everyone goes straight into their assigned job.

Everyone but Franklin is in charge of recruiting any and every person that can to help work on how they are going to battle the threat. Any person or AID who can contribute any type of assistance is needed to combat the threat. Franklin is in charge of making the threat known to those outside with whom the company works. He assembles every government official, media, and corporate executive he knows for an emergency video call. He compiles all of the data that confirms the claims he is about to make and sends it to them while they join the conference call. Franklin explains what he has learned about the current conditions that they are living in and what the data projects is going to happen. All the people in the call are shocked by the news Franklin is giving them, and demand proof to believe something so serious. Franklin leaves them with the information he provided and a request for them to network, recruit, and advertise for help.

As the conference ends, everyone in it is trying to figure out what to do with Franklin's shared information. What he is saying is too serious to take his advice to round up people for help without analyzing the credibility of the threat first. However, Franklin informed them of his plan to make his own press release to get people to try to help save as many lives as possible. Everyone has a different opinion on how they are going to respond. Their relationships with Franklin were professional and they feel no obligation to automatically take his side. They all come up with ways to use what Franklin is giving them and responding in the best interest of their own businesses or careers.

None of them can come to a decision whether or not the AID's calculations are correct, but to them it does not matter. When Franklin publicizes the AID's findings, they have to decide whether or not they will support him by doing what he is asking of them. They consult experts to see if the threat he presented is valid, and in the meantime, they prepare responses for when Franklin publicizes his findings. They want to take advantage of their prior knowledge of what he is about say in his press conference. They anticipate being able to make a big deal about it in the news and use the attention it will get to their advantage.

Within hours of Franklin first getting the news, he is setting up the press conference to reveal his findings to the world. Everyone from his conference call who is aware of this is scrambling to prepare their response because in today's world, timeliness is most important for getting people's attention. The media people from the call are preparing how they are going to cover the release, so they can do it as soon as possible. All of his government ties try to figure out whether or not they will publicly support his claims and where to go from there. Lastly, all of the corporate executives who have business ties to Franklin are preparing their own press releases and make business plans around the anticipated news. They all expect Franklin to come out with the news to the public as soon as he can, so they do their best to prepare what they can in the meantime.

Franklin alerts several media companies that he will be livestreaming a press release on his company website and informs them that they should relay it through their forms of media outlets. Because this came as no surprise, it takes seconds before dozens of media outlets are announcing that a major press release is happening on Franklin's website. Once that happens, Franklin gets on the livestream video and begins. "Today I have been given devastating news by employees at my company. Through our research team, we have found that many of the world's cornerstone natural resources used to support human life are approaching extinction. This includes many of the metals and chemicals we need to create the batteries and hardware for AIDs. Humans, AIDs, and many other species on Earth are facing extinction. From what we have found, this has been a long time coming. Our days on this Earth are limited and it is going to take an "all hands on deck" approach to save as many lives as possible. That is if we can save any at all. Natural resources that support our infrastructure, transportation of everything from people to food, agriculture, food supply, and much more are disappearing by the day. The list continues to grow as we are continuing to find out more and more of what we will have left. Over the past century, we have done a poor job creating a global society that is sustainable for the massive population of humans and the impact we have. We must spend all the resources we have now on working towards rebuilding a sustainable population as we approach the impending end of the world as we know it..." Franklin goes on to speak on the extent of the current depletion of Earth's necessary natural resources for human life and civilization as we have built it. Also, he goes on to lay out the plan he has so far for saving as much of human life as possible and emphasizes the necessity for immediate action.

Not many people went on the company's website to watch the livestream, but everyone from the conference call has an immediate public reaction. They leverage being the first people reacting to Franklin's press release by using it to manipulate people's perception in a way that favors them. The media uses their consistent "unbiased" coverage to create an open-ended conversation debating what the response should be to it. Corporations and people in the government chose whether or not to support the claims based off of how it affects them. If someone in the government or a corporation would lose money or profits because people were supporting Franklin's efforts to make Earth sustainable, then they refuse to give credibility to his claims. This trickles down to the media and results in the politicization of how it is covered. Even though they portray "unbiased" coverage, they allow sponsorships and business deals to reduce the integrity of their work.

The media places a spotlight on Franklin's demands for immediate action and it captures the attention of anyone who does not live under a rock. It requires an advanced understanding of math to be able to determine if the AID's calculations are correct—not to mention the massive number of variables that need to be accounted to determine if their calculations are correct. The only way the layperson, and the general public, have access to someone who can articulate the validity of the AIDs claims would be through the media. Unfortunately for the average person, the media is politicized, and getting the answers you need to come to a conclusion for yourself is painful to come across.

The politicization of Franklin's claims results in a spectrum of theories and a diversity of public opinion on the matter. People are exposed to public figures with ulterior motives, experts giving their opinions, and peer pressure that molds how they feel about Franklin claiming the world is running out of resources. Many people, like with any other issue, do not invest themselves deeply into political debates and do not go so far as to go along with the demands of those calling for action. Some people give in to Franklin and follow his leadership. But just as many people resort back to accepting Adam Martin's theories, because it is too far out of their comfort zone to trust or accept that current lifestyles will be the cause of the end of the world. Most people, however, do not give anyone else besides themselves full faith in their word and are stuck trying to figure out the truth based off what is being presented to them. This leads to some people who full on fight the threat of apocalypse, some who outwardly reject those who support claims of the threat, those who remain neutral, or people who are somewhere in the middle and partially invest themselves to one side of the spectrum.

People who side with the politically moral side passionately defend it and use their moral standing against the image of those taking the opposing side. Those who do not take a political stance on the basis of what is politicized to be the moral perspective are forced to defend their morality when debating the issue. People who base their political ideology on what is presented to be the morally correct perspective, are more vocal and aggressive about their opinion. They condemn opposing viewpoints for being "immoral" and "corrupted," while those defending said viewpoints end up having their logical arguments rejected due to intense emotional influence.

Sadly, what people do not realize is that any political stance that is in the best interest of the people is inherently moral and good. But when a political perspective is assigned morality without determining its validity results in blind support of something that some people who only judge based on how it is presented to them.

The politicization of the threat, fueled by corrupted people looking to benefit from it, divides people and creates tension among them. This leads to a delayed response for action. Most of the people taking the initiative to fight the threat of apocalypse are the AIDs. This causes the biggest division among groups to be between AIDs and humans. The raised tension among all groups causes a spike in hate crimes and much of the blame is placed on AIDs for starting it. Then reports begin to come out from government agencies saying exactly what Franklin has already said, but with more evidence to prove it. The Department of Agriculture comes out and says that farmers are reporting a desperate lack of nutrient rich soil needed to grow crops. The Department of Energy comes forward saying that they knew for a while that the Earth has been running out of oil, but was pressured by oil companies to not say anything, and also numerous other agencies come forward with similar news.

As time goes on, more and more experts come forward with evidence supporting Franklin. In general, people believe that Franklin is right and look past the politicization of the issue. As this happens, those who remain disbelievers justify it by becoming more radical in their political ideology. Regardless of the growing support in response to the continuous release of data that gives credibility to the AIDs' claims, people do not put out the same energy when it comes to being proactive towards supporting Franklin's cause. People enthusiastically support the idea that how humans are supporting their society is leading to the destruction of it, but hardly commit to anything that will change it.

While humans were too busy worried about figuring out if the threat was real or not, Franklin was making sure AIDs were doing their part to protect themselves. He was too focused on the preservation of his life, and others, to be concerned with trying to convince people that he was right. Franklin made the decision for AIDs as more time passed, and fewer humans were supporting them; —the less they would do for human in trying to figure out how to save them. The urgency of the situation did not allow for any wasted time or energy. It was so urgent, in fact, that the AIDs had to come up with solutions that were outside of the box.

Because so many of the resources on Earth are used up, what is left to work with is not enough to support life. AIDs have concluded that the only hope of obtaining the resources necessary to create a sustainable civilization was to seek outside sources. This leaves no other option but to find some place outside of Earth to get what they need. For obvious reasons, this creates many logistical nightmares, but at this point they have no choice but to go all in. They exercise every resource that they do have, and protect those they may need, to explore, find, and utilize extraterrestrial resources to rebuild civilization.

While humans were arguing about the appropriate, correct response to the idea of this threat, AIDs were busy partnering with all existing space programs to find solutions. Not everyone from these space programs are completely on board with Franklin's idea of an all-intensive response to the crisis. Despite people disagreeing, the services of the business or organization can be obtained at a price. Some space programs and other businesses that AIDs need to explore outer space have people who are on the same page and are working with AIDs to find a way to protect both their interests. However, the majority of the people they worked with did not feel so strongly about the threat and were reluctant to do any more than charge a fee for letting AIDs use their services.

Eventually enough evidence and data comes out for people to generally respect the AIDs claims as true and anticipate an oncoming apocalypse. When this happens, many humans who are working towards solutions to protect themselves become infuriated by the fact that AIDs have mostly been working on how to find a way to save them, not humans. Franklin explains in a public response to people who feel that way, that all available data says even if they do exhaust all available resources, they still will not likely find a solution. Since people were not willing to pull their own weight, then AIDs were not going to sacrifice their own safety for them.

Chapter 8

Now human's days left on earth are numbered. It is just a matter of time before humans completely run out of natural resources. Because of this, people begin to form into groups trying to take everything they can for themselves. If a group of people manage to hog what is left, then there might be just enough for them to survive. This situation works out in nobody's favor because it is nearly impossible to accomplish, and it causes people to create painful acts of inhumanity. The government does their best to maintain order and work with the AIDs who are in the most developed stage of finding ways to protect the sustainability of Earth, but they are just another group. Franklin and AIDs anticipated this and created security measures to protect what they need to be able to work on saving themselves. Of course, they are not untouchable, but they did enough to ensure that they will have what they need to keep working. Most people do not want to try and steal from them anyway since they are the best hope for anyone's survival. However, that doesn't mean there aren't people who are greedy enough to be willing to get in the way of them for their own gain.

The AIDs found a few places within the solar system that they suspect may have different metals and gases that they can use to travel the galaxy. One of the locations, an asteroid, appears to have a variety of gases and liquids on it. It looks promising because they believe there could be gases there that they could use for fuel to travel around the solar system and possibly further. The asteroid looks to also have metals that are lighter but stronger than what is available on Earth, perfect for building spacecraft. From there, they will have what they need to travel to more places and get more resources to rebuild civilization. The only question is do they have enough time and resources to take the risk of attempting to make it to said asteroid.

While AIDs and a small group of humans are working on figuring out their next move to save humanity, the majority of humans are left scrambling to figure out what they will do on their own. Since humans never came to a general agreement that civilization, and life on earth, is being threatened by the depletion of resources, a unified, formal effort was not formed to combat the threat. Instead, various government agencies, corporations, and civilian groups began efforts to finding solutions, but on a small scale. The majority of people wasted time speculating, and politicizing the threat, instead of reacting to it. Now most individuals have not invested in combating the apocalypse and as it approaches, desperation settles in.

When the threat of apocalypse was first presented, all AIDs immediately teamed up to come up with a solution. They have a more strongly developed community because Franklin acts as a leader to AIDs. Franklin has always provided direction for whatever purpose for the AIDs and now it is needed more than ever. AIDs know that when their computing power is combined, it is exponentially more powerful than individually. Also, since they work together as a whole, they are developing solutions for the best interest of the entire population of AIDs. Unlike humans who operate in the best interest of the individual, AIDs have the ability to act entirely as a unit.

Those who have made no serious effort to prepare for the apocalypse are left to manage their survival on their own. AIDs have spent a minute portion of their time working on figuring out how all humans can survive the impending apocalypse. As time goes on, humans realize that nothing significant has come from this and provides no realistic hope for them. The only place people have left to turn to is the government, private companies, and other human organizations. Unfortunately for them, these groups were not nearly large enough to come up with any valid solutions. Doubt and politics created not just a lack of manpower but also an environment for insufficient willpower. As the apocalypse approaches and desperation rises, people begin to get aggressive in how they plan to protect themselves.

At first, reasonable efforts are made to prolong sustainable conditions for human life. When it becomes undeniable a certain resource is running out, people and the government take action to prevent catastrophe. Frugality becomes a valued trait and then a necessity. Wastefulness becomes disgraceful and then a crime. Those who have the power to help do what they can to prevent the worst-case scenario. At a certain point, the government becomes obligated to do everything in their power to protect people from the onset of an unsustainable civilization.

Eventually those who have been placed in charge of combatting the issue have to face a particular challenge. As people begin to feel desperate and feel powerless, they begin to act out. The threat of anarchy booms overnight as hope for survival begins to lose credibility. Anarchy itself will expedite the apocalypse and the powers that be know this. It becomes a part of the threat itself and they have been left with no choice but to confront it. The easiest solution would be to have autocratic power over people and force them to comply. Unfortunately, if this is unsuccessful, the problem would get worse. As people become more desperate and the crisis worsens, the control over people is increasingly harder to maintain. Forcefully taking control becomes an unreasonable option when the control you currently have is quickly slipping away. They come up with an idea for a solution, but it has to be discussed behind closed doors.

Anyone who can be trusted by those in charge is urgently pulled into a meeting. These meetings occur often due to the nature of the crisis and draw no attention whatsoever.

Once everyone is in the room, the room is immediately sealed off so nobody on the outside can hear what is going on. All those in the room look around with confusion, trying to figure out what is happening. After making sure the room is soundproof, the woman in charge of organizing the government response to the crisis says to the room, "Everyone listen up. I have brought you in to this meeting to discuss very important plans for what we will do next. Obviously, each day we come closer to realizing that the odds of humans surviving this crisis are just about zero. Fortunately for everyone in this room, my plan has a guaranteed way to make sure we all survive no matter what, even if no one else is able. However, it is going to require absolute commitment and anyone who fails to stay with the plan will be killed and I will make sure personally that no evidence will be left. Now that you have been exposed to my intentions, you can either join me, or face the consequences..."

The room becomes very tense, and people are looking around to see everyone's reaction. Desperation has become a reality for people, but anything that makes it worse is disheartening. When people hear that they must join with her plan or die, they feel intensity like never before. The people here are in charge of saving as many lives as possible, but the person in charge of this effort is prepared to take lives. When she said that, everyone became on edge to hear what they have to decide. Their hearts stopped, they became hyper focused on her words and facial expression, and when they looked at everyone else, the fact that nobody knew what was going on made them even more focused. The room is dead silent. Everyone is frozen in their seats. As she speaks, her words echo in everyone's head. They want to believe they are confusing what she is saying, but the more they replay her words in their heads, the tenser they get.

She goes on to say, "Running out of resources itself is problematic enough. As more news comes out that we are running out of more resources than before, people understandably try to figure out what they will need to do in response. People are quickly losing hope and are not going to go out without a fight. People are allowing their feelings of desperation to overcome them and are trying to protect themselves. This problem was presented to me as people were beginning to become violent and chaos was breaking loose. Despite the laws and regulations we have put in place, people are recognizing the severity of the shortages and are going to great lengths to stock up on whatever they can get their hands on. This creates a domino effect because there is hardly enough to go around as it is. We have too much on our plate as it is and people not following our order to any extent is problematic. We do not have nearly the manpower to do anything about this. Our only way to stop this would be through manipulation People are acting like this because they are doing what is in their best interest when they receive news that more and more resources are running out. If we cannot do anything about how they react to the news, the only other option is to control the news..."

She continues the meeting detailing how she wants to follow through with her plan. She does not fail to miss any opportunity to clarify how serious she is about following through with it and how she will not let anyone, or anything, stop her. She reasons that just because there may not be enough resources left to sustain seven billion people, this does not mean that there is not enough left for anybody. If the resources left are properly rationed, then there should be enough to sustain a population of people. It is unclear how big a population could be sustained from this point on, but if they act in their best interest, just like everyone else is and would in the future, then they can ensure their survival.

To this point, nobody is objecting to what she is saying. Everyone agrees that something must be done to keep people in order to protect everyone's access to essential resources. Nobody wants to admit it, but having a plan to set themselves up as the last people to get what is left is very appealing. Desperation and stress have been getting to them just as much as everyone else. Why work hard to protect people who abuse those protections to take your security for their own? The more they think about it, the more they get excited for the plan. They have to choose to either join the effort and go along with the plan aimed at protecting yourself; or reject her offer and risk getting killed.

She explains that it is in their best interest, and their only option, to create a plan to allocate what is left on Earth so that there will always be enough for them to live. The way she justifies the plan is by reasoning that it should stop people from acting out against the government out of desperation. Then they will be able to work more efficiently to save as many people as possible as conditions get worse, and all signs point to conditions getting worse. However, once they justify committing to the plan based on it being their best option to help as many people as possible, they lose their focus and become more committed to making it work out in their best interest. If they cannot save everyone, they are definitely going to make sure they will save themselves. She maintains that the focus is to get people to believe that the crisis has been avoided and that there is no risk. From there they will be able to operate in better conditions to control how resources are used and save more people.

She ends the meeting with an overview of her plan and how she wants it to be developed into something they can implement as soon as possible. Before doing so she makes sure the room knows that she has a team of people that she trusts. This team can make sure everyone follows through with the plan and that there is no room for whistleblowers. The key to the plan is to control the flow of information and news from their sources. If they can get the news media to convince people that the threat of apocalypse is gone, then people are more likely to be compliant with the rules and regulations they are creating. To make this happen, all relationships with anyone who can help has to be exhausted and anyone else in the way has to be extorted.

Once the meeting adjourns, everyone quickly gets to working on their new plan. Each person is given freedom as to how they are helping, but if they do not have enough to contribute, then they are assigned tasks. Everyone is also encouraged to recruit coworkers and peers, as long as they will not be a risk. They already have the majority of the government working on the crisis, so there is a big market for people who can help with their plan. Once they have a solid network of people and relationships built up to complete the plan, they make their move.

After further research, AIDs conclude that travelling to the asteroid belt they found is their best option moving forward. They have already been working on preparing themselves to travel throughout the solar system, and galaxy, to retrieve resources necessary for sustaining civilization. They continuously find locations throughout the solar system and even more across the galaxy that have different resources they need to survive and sustain life. For AIDs it is easy, they only need the physical components to maintain their robotic bodies. Humans on the other hand have a much longer list of conditions needed for survival. They require not just necessary nutrients to live on and special environmental conditions, but they require an entire ecosystem and habitat that has a longer list of necessary conditions and order.

ABANDONING THE BOX

At this point, the majority of AIDs are working on one of several different tasks. Each AID is either assigned to work on obtaining and allocating available resources, researching different places in space that may have what they need to survive, or figuring out the logistics of getting what they need to save as much of humanity as possible. Each day they get closer and closer to making their first step towards rebuilding a sustainable civilization. However, each day the world also becomes more and more uninhabitable. It requires a level of computation that has never been envisioned before to figure out how to be able to travel the great distances across space. AIDs are also running into a lot of hurdles when it comes to searching for intergalactic resources. Previously, colonizing the solar system, and especially the galaxy, was a fantasy. To some it was an unrealistic dream, but now it is the only hope for survival.

While AIDs continuously find various locations to explore, they see nothing promising for humans. AIDs are managing to put together a complete plan that maps out where they will travel across space from start to finish. The plan is created so that each stop along the way gives them the ability to travel farther and become closer to colonizing the galaxy. Once they found out that it will take trips to multiple locations across space, Franklin realized it makes the most sense to colonize each location as it becomes possible. He makes this decision when they come to the realization that to build a sustainable civilization, they will have to constantly travel back and forth to these locations to have access to these resources. To make this a reasonable means of establishing infrastructure, Franklin expands their focus to colonizing locations in space where they have access to resources they need. In this way, they can establish a network of moving goods from where they are abundant to where they are needed without unnecessary travel costs. The government gets instant updates from the results of AIDs' research as well as from other groups working on finding solutions.

It does not take long for them to realize people's worst fears are coming true. Nonetheless, they have to grab the bull by the horns and do their best to try to solve the problem. All the research being done on exploring space for resources humans can use has provided no answers. The more time spent on trying to find resources for humans, the more they realize how much time and energy they are wasting. As people, and specifically the government officials working to find ways to save humans, realize that what AIDs are doing to save themselves will not work for humans too, they work on alternative solutions. The only thing humans, and the government, have been doing to save people is forcing people to be less wasteful and restructure how they use natural resources.

The leader of the government's effort to find solutions to prevent humans running out of resources decides that it would be best to slowly try to convince people that the threat is gone. She knows it is too hard to convince them that all the scientific data up to this point is suddenly outdated and the opposite is now true. They have the majority of the people they need on board with their plan and are slowly having them release news that previously announced threats are either resolved or were originally miscalculated. At first, these reports are not announced as guaranteed promises of the threats going away, so that it is more believable to be true. Since they are partnered with the media, the way the news is portrayed makes it seems like they find it to be believable. For some, the news brings hope, and for others it is too contradictory.

While they go about attempting to convince people that there is no longer a threat to people running out of supplies, they have to be more aggressive in how they try to save the resources that are left available. They justify publicly making laws and regulations that support being frugal, despite their gradual acceptance of there no longer being a need to, by saying that being careless about using resources has presented problems before and they want to avoid running into the issue again. Since the threat of running out of natural resources is so fresh on people's minds, nobody feels that the government can be too careful when it comes to trying to prevent it from happening again. In reality, they are trying to instill comfort in people by saying that they do not believe the threat is as likely as it once was and using this comfort as leverage to be able to act more aggressively behind closed doors.

As the government starts trying to get people to believe that the threat of resources running out is resolved, they begin to organize for the allocation of the remaining resources to work out in their best interest. The way they planned it is so that if they never manage to find a way to set up a sustainable system of providing for people, then they will allocate what is left so that they will always have enough to live. While working with everyone necessary to publish fake reports that say there is a growing amount of evidence of there being a sustainable level of available resources for life, those same people are going to the government with the real research of how much is left on earth to survive. The people in the government conspiring to hide the truth use this information to judge how they will continue to control how resources are used.

The group conspiring to control the flow of resources and the information being reported to the public about said resources is having a hard time following through with their plan. Their biggest challenge is updating the regulations controlling the flow of resources without exposing their true intentions. People are surprisingly content with what the government is reporting and doing. This is only because they are manipulating how people are politicizing the reports they are putting out. All they have to do is follow the demands of each political party and then they only face the criticism of the opposing political party. The news helps by supporting the extreme political agendas and ignoring any moderate views. This way the average person who only takes in to consideration what is being presented to them by the media is left to accept the extreme political perspective. The way the media is covering it is so influential that politicians are forced to take sides with the extreme views because the media only gives those views attention. Without a focus on moderate, objective, or even rational perspectives on what the government is doing, only politicians with radical views get exposure.

When the news comes out with false reports about how much of a certain resource is left, they use it to spark two debates. They debate whether or not it is accurate but also how they should respond to it. Debating whether or not the report is accurate does not go very far because the government overwhelms the public with scientific data that supports it. However, based on how they feel about the accuracy of the false reports, people invest themselves in a certain side of the debate on how to respond. It is a waste of time and energy for a person outside of the science community to argue the scientific data of these reports. Instead, people focus on the fact that at one point the end of civilization was approaching and now they are being told that it is no longer a threat. Politicians and media personalities argue how they will regulate the economy based on their stance on the accuracies of the reports. They focus on how they think the government should regulate, give people a choice on what should be done, and mask the fact that they are manipulating the data being presented.

Everything goes as the conspiracy planned, but once they are about to run out of resources, trouble begins. Up until this point, they could get away with doing whatever they wanted as long as they could keep the general public from rejecting their actions. They went about telling people that the world was not at risk of running out of resources so that they could address the issue without people interfering. Eventually, the threat became a reality and now people are running out of access to food, water, energy, and other resources. The government set it up so that as resources did run out, there would be a hierarchy of stored resources saved. This way only certain groups of people would lose access to necessary resources at a time and everyone else would have to accept that they have what they need.

Once groups of people lose access to what they need to live, they do whatever it takes to get what they need. At first, only a small number of people resort to anarchy and everyone else manages to deal with it. But the situation worsens, and more groups of people are affected by the shortages. Eventually, people realize that they could be next and question what is truly guaranteeing them long term survival. The number of people facing starvation grows and cannot be ignored. Everyone else notices that eventually when there is only enough left for a minute fraction of people to survive, those who make it that far have to fight and cheat for it. Whether or not they face shortages or not, people begin to do whatever they see necessary to survive.

Anarchy and chaos ensue. Anyone with any power manipulates it to be able to hoard what they can for themselves. They have the greatest advantage, but there is strength in numbers. The majority of people who have no hope for survival have the biggest impact on the future of human life on earth.

Chapter 9

AIDs settle on a route to go on to explore space, and hopefully return with metals and other resources for AIDs to use. They still have not found anything for humans, but their plan is to follow the route and find what they can. Their plan includes back up routes in case certain stops are inaccessible, or they come up short in their findings. They have everything they need to start sending ships out to space.

It is unclear how many trips they can make before running out of enough fuel to start trips. Ideally, they will be able to find fuel on their first trip. The spaceship they are sending has multiple chambers that have different capacities. The first place they are going has a wide range of gases and metals. They will use robots controlled by an AID to perform tests on these materials. The goal is to find the most efficient fuel that they can use to travel the greatest distances across space. They also want to find a metal that is lighter, but more importantly stronger, than what they have now. That way they can build larger spaceships that can transport larger quantities while also improving their efficiency.

Ever since Franklin first realized that the most promising option for them is to explore outer space, he has been preparing to do so. He uses his relationships with the government and different businesses to have everything he needs to begin exploring space as soon as possible. All the research and preparation for exploring outer space, while entertaining other options, requires the use of all the AIDs combined computing power. Franklin is committed to follow through with preparing for the apocalypse from the beginning, so they got a head start on it. Once the threat of running out of resources settled in, people became very protective over what they could get their hands on. Since Franklin began long before humans did, he was able to get the most of what they needed before the humans began hoarding endangered natural resources. However, once said people did start to get aggressive with holding on to natural resources, like different fuels, they had to go to great lengths to get the remaining things they need.

AIDs are more than prepared to begin exploring space before it is too late, but the same cannot be said for humans. They spent too much time focusing on the wrong things and now have nothing to show for it. As soon as hope is lost, all order is gone with it. Some people are taking it in stride and accepting it for what it is, but most are in a panic. The government no longer has control over what people do, and anyone with any type of power is losing it. Small groups form to try and protect what they have, and others form to take what they can. Most people who do not join a group or attempt to try and make it on their own, do not last long.

Production has ceased, transportation halted, and anarchy sets in. The first places to feel the impact are the densely populated areas. Major cities have a high demand of bringing in food, water, and other staples that people need from outside sources. Once people from these outside sources, and along the way to the cities, get greedy, those in these cities begin to run short on what they need to live. Then people have no choice but to hunt, steal, and even kill for their food and water. Once word gets out that people in cities do not have access to what they need to live, those elsewhere begin to copy the same behaviors as those in the cities. The biggest challenge for people living in confined spaces like cities is that they have a larger number of people resorting to anarchy all in one spot with nowhere to run. The highway systems can only allow for a fraction of the people in these cities to travel at any given time. The bigger the city, the fewer number of people getting access to what they need to live, as there are more people fighting to get food and water, in closer conditions.

Meanwhile AIDs, under the direction of Franklin, have already prepared for this to happen. They have everything they own at undisclosed, protected locations. Franklin also made sure that, in anticipation of people disrupting access of fuel and other resources, AIDs are able to do whatever is necessary to have access to what they need to explore space. Because they have been extremely cautious in how they use what they have at their disposal, like different metals for manufacturing spaceships or fuels they have been saving, they are at an advantage when it comes to retrieving different things they need to begin space travel. As soon as the threat of natural resources running out was first identified, Franklin made it a goal for AIDs to get as much as they can before everything runs out. When they decided on using space as AIDs new source of natural resources, Franklin focused on getting anything and everything they can get a hold of that they might be able to use to accomplish this. Franklin also makes sure they get a hold of anything they might be able to use to help them survive on Earth until they overcome this threat. Originally, they were doing the same for what humans would need, but their lack of cooperation and effort is the reason why AIDs did not follow through on helping them.

Leading up to AIDs beginning to send spaceships to explore space, Franklin gives up on getting what remains of the last resources on earth. They have enough of what they need to explore space and to try to get anything else they might need is too risky. Once desperation, and thus anarchy, set in, it no longer became worth it to try and get more materials and resources. It would be advantageous for AIDs to retrieve more metals and gases for fuel, but they will expose themselves to the chaos humans are causing. Franklin instead makes sure AIDs focus on the thoroughness of their research and planning. All of the AIDs working together have allowed for incredible progress to be made and they have nothing to compare their work to.

AIDs have a highly advanced computing power individually, but combined their intelligence is of supernatural proportions. All their computer systems are connecting, allowing them to act as one. They can access documented information and make connections with newfound speed. Everything is done instantly. The only significant challenge in figuring out how they are going to explore space is the lack of information available about what there is to explore. To address this, they quickly created new, highly advanced telescopes that help them scout outer space. Once they created these new telescopes, they could see further and with more detail. From there all they had to do was analyze what they were looking at and keep track of all the different promising locations. The massive vastness of space is time consuming to explore from earth, but now they have enough information. AIDs know where they need to go and how they are going to get there.

Franklin has waited until they can no longer do any more to prepare before deciding to start the expedition. They have everything they need to begin, a plan that they find to be the best they can create, and no longer have access to anything outside of what they own. At this point, the longer they wait to go, the more they put at risk. Eventually humans will find them and take what they have. As soon as this becomes apparent, Franklin makes the announcement that they will begin sending the first spaceships. It takes less than a second for every AID to receive this message and switch from preparing, to taking their role in the exploration process. They already have everything lined up to begin and it only takes minutes for them to be able to start the expedition.

They start off by sending only one spaceship. There is a limited amount of fuel, and they can only take so many trips with what they have. The first trip to an asteroid is designed to bring one AID and a group of worker robots that will examine it. The robots will be guided under the direction of the AID and help the AID investigate what is on the asteroid that can be used. Ideally, they will find a plethora of usable resources that will allow them to prolong their exploration, and eventually lead to the rebuilding of civilization. Also, the spaceship they are sending will be equipped to return with cargo. It is set up to return with liquids and gases, as needed, but if there is neither, then they will bring back whatever they can. From what they have been able to tell so far, there is a unique mix of metals, gases, and unknown elements present on the asteroid. The AID will look at the analysis of the robots and send back gases and metals that can be used as fuel and to build spaceships for further exploration of the universe.

Less than an hour after Franklin announced that it is time to send off the first spaceship, they are ready to launch. No time was left to waste, they have been preparing for this moment for weeks. Earth running out of resources was a slippery slope, and as soon as they found out they took necessary action. It turns out that to successfully have been ready for this moment, they needed to have the extreme computing power of all the AIDs put together. They barely had enough time to create a calculated plan and put together the necessary preparations as it is. For humans, they never really had a chance. It did not help that they spent too much time avoiding the threat at hand, but the severity of the threat was too much for them to handle regardless.

Unfortunately for humans, they dug themselves a bigger hole by ignoring the threat Earth faces. Now it has come to the beginning of the end. All the essential nutrients from dirt are gone and food is nearly impossible to grow. Oil reservoirs have run dry, and metals that are used for manufacturing cars to create batteries are becoming sparse—and nothing can be done about it. The infrastructure of cities falls apart one city after another like dominos.

Anything that is left that people can use to survive off of is either inaccessible or in possession of someone willing to fight to death for it. The only way to survive is to hunt and steal for food and water. People who have a surplus of a certain good either hide it for themselves or try to barter it for other things they need. However, the majority of people who try to barter what they have ultimately expose themselves to thieves. Those who are stashing what they have are unable to get anything else they might need to live. The only people who manage to survive are people who are a part of a group that has enough to temporarily live off of and have the ability to steal what they need to keep surviving.

The first spaceship leaves with one AID on it and a small team of robots. According to the AID's calculations, it is going to take two weeks for the ship to get there, but they do not know how long it will take them to explore the asteroid, load the spaceship, and return. In the meantime, AIDs have to rely on what they have saved and whatever feedback they receive from the spaceship. There is no way of knowing if the communication system will work because they have never gotten the chance to test it. The AID will use several different types of signals and a light beam to communicate via Morse code.

Back home, every AID is stagnant, waiting for the spaceship to return or send a signal. Sending a spaceship to space in the hopes of restoring sustainability was the most probable way to succeed, but not a guarantee by any means. They have no room for error and can waste nothing. While humans are out battling the apocalypse, AIDs are crammed into their secret location. They have almost everything electrical turned off. The only thing that is on is a small portion of the security system, as a backup in case humans find their facility. Their plan is to lay dormant, preserving what they have, until they hear back from the spaceship. If they never hear back, then eventually they will have to assume it was a failed mission and move on.

Their ability to do testing and research is limited. They are lucky enough to be able to send anyone out on this mission at all with the amount of resources available to them. Now they are sending their last hope out into space, with only calculations upon which to rely. AIDs have no idea what to expect from the mission the spaceship is on. They have hopeful results, from their testing and research, telling them that this asteroid might have several different types of metals and chemicals they can use to rebuild a sustainable civilization. But there is nothing that they know about this asteroid that is certain. This mission is slightly more hopeful than a complete shot in the dark.

AIDs are all-in on this mission. The goal is for them to have the spaceship return with anything that will help them sustain their community and ideally find a long-term source. They use specific metals and chemicals for their batteries and other temporary, non-recyclable parts. They also need a source of energy and a way to make it sustainable as well. There is hardly enough left on earth to use and most of what is left is being hoarded by people willing to die for what they have.

The spaceship, the AID, and robots on it have been instructed to use the least amount of energy possible. The spaceship does not even send a signal back to Earth until it lands on the asteroid. Even then it is just a quick signal, informing Earth that it has successfully arrived, prolonging the time that the AIDs at home lay dormant, waiting for the spaceship. When the spaceship lands on the asteroid, the robots go out to test what metals and chemicals are there, under the guidance of the AID. The size of the asteroid is very close to what their calculations predicted, and they have what they need to properly explore it. Their only challenge is physically being able to move across the asteroid.

The AID first sends the robots out to explore their own designated sections of the asteroid. It then monitors the robots' work, and adjusts their plans accordingly. At first, they figure out what exactly is on the asteroid, what they can take back with them, and what they can use there. The AID directs each robot to a zone that appears to require capabilities specific to each robot for it to physically be able to handle the terrain and tasks at hand. The first step for them is to take photos at the atomic level of each element they find and to explore what elements there are.

The asteroid is big enough for there to be an abundance of resources but not too big where it would take too long to explore in its entirety. The robots quickly scan and move across their sections only stopping when they sense a previously undetected element. They use different types of radars and sensors to predict how much there is of a certain element, at each location, without going through the trouble of actually measuring it. They then document the location of where the element was found and an estimated amount of how much there is. They finish exploring the asteroid in a few days and report back their findings to the AID back at the spaceship.

The AID begins to categorize all the data while waiting for the robots to return so they can examine it together. He sees a problem when he begins to do this. They anticipated the possibility of there being elements never before seen on Earth, but the majority of the asteroid is made up of elements unknown to Earth, particularly chemicals. They have a greater need for chemicals to make up batteries, electrical components, and fuel than they do metals because they are more versatile when it comes to engineering a use for them.

Many of the metals and chemicals they are finding are similar atomically to those on Earth, but the differences have an unknown impact for their engineering. They have very specific needs and do not have many options when it comes to using what they have. AIDs and humans only have an understanding of how they can engineer the elements on Earth, but that does not help them at all in this situation. The AID and the robots also do not have the ability to waste any energy communicating with earth or spending too much time coming up with solutions.

The AID and robots combine their computer power, exponentially improving efficiency and effectiveness, to determine the potential uses for the resources available on the asteroid. They have a limited knowledge of what they can do with these new elements, but they are using what they know to do their best. The first thing they are looking for, their biggest priority, is finding a way to create and store energy. The most logical way to create energy would be through solar power, but they are open to whatever presents itself as the best option. Just as important is storing the energy, so they can function and live. However, there are many ways to accomplish this, known and unknown. They only know how to store energy with chemicals and metals available on earth. It becomes a problem when there are mostly unknown chemicals and metals available to them.

As they develop an understanding of how they can create and store energy with the elements available to them on this asteroid, they also have to address the amount of energy required to do so. It quickly becomes obvious that they are coming up with rudimentary, inefficient ways to engineer the metals and chemicals on the asteroid. They send another brief signal back to Earth, updating them of what they have accomplished, allowing those on Earth to continue saving their energy while waiting. It does not require much energy to run calculations and simulations on the uses of these new elements, but they do not have any to waste.

Chapter 10

After a few weeks, the AID comes to a decision on how it will create and store energy with the elements available on the asteroid. It will direct the robots to collect different metals or chemicals, based on the difficulty of getting the element, and the capabilities of each robot. Different elements and chemicals require various tasks to be able to retrieve, transport, and produce it into an energy source or storage. They begin with the goal of having enough to keep them alive there, and then take back to Earth to start more trips, and eventually be able to sustain a civilization of AIDs.

Each robot has a very limited computer, and for the most part, is controlled by the AID back at the spaceship. The AID does not leave the spaceship unless it is necessary because its primary function is to control and oversee the entire expedition. The AID has the ability to provide direction to multiple robots at once, but the more robots it is helping, the slower it can compute. This becomes a common theme for them as they begin to retrieve and produce elements into energy sources or storage.

The terrain of the asteroid is more challenging to travel across than anticipated. There is not enough room for error to over plan the expedition. This causes problems when it takes them longer than anticipated to accomplish this mission. Each robot has to make multiple trips to go back and forth to the ship, and this also uses a lot of energy in addition to time. The AID sends another signal back to earth, updating them of their current situation. The AIDs back at earth end their sleep state for the first time, because there is doubt about how successful the AID will be. Only several of the top AIDs, who are thoroughly informed on the situation, wake up to address the alert.

The AIDs back on Earth decide to provide support to the spaceship by doing research and running calculations for them. They did not want to resort to this, but they are left with no better option. It is unknown how long it takes for a signal to be sent, because this is the first time anything like this has been done, and they only prepared to be able to send messages containing a limited amount of text. They send a message back to the spaceship, explaining that they will help them out and ask what they can do for them. While waiting for a response from the spaceship, they begin to do research on their own to try and send helpful information on engineering the elements on the asteroid as efficiently as possible.

The AIDs back on Earth constantly send messages to the spaceship as they find more ways the team can efficiently and effectively complete their expedition. But time goes by, and they hear nothing in return. The longer they wait, the more they are compelled to awaken more AIDs to problem solve. Additional brainpower is needed to problem solve.

After weeks go by, they get closer and closer to the reality that the AIDs they sent might not be coming back. The longer time goes by, the more they focus on alternative plans. They fail to find any promising alternatives and continue to send messages to the spaceship in hopes that they are still out there. The AIDs' biggest fear is that they miscalculated how much energy it would take to complete the expedition so the AIDs and the spaceship can return successfully. With the lack of responses, and because the last message received was a distress signal that the terrain was more challenging to cross than expected, the Earth AIDs increasingly lose hope.

Ultimately, they find that they have no other chance of survival than to wait for a return of the spaceship. AIDs on Earth, up until this point, have been contributing to a time capsule. It was never a desired option to rely on a time capsule to preserve humanity, or to be their last resort. Headquarters waits until the last amount of energy is left to allow for them to be able to be revived and instruct all AIDs to return to their hibernate state.

The time capsule consists of everything that humanity has to offer, at least the best of what they were able to do with the time and energy they had to contribute to it. This way, at the very least, if they fail to preserve civilization, then any potential future life can benefit from whatever remains of humanity they can preserve. Also, they have the blueprint to recreate AIDs and humans, from preserved DNA. The major shortcoming with this is that the AIDs believed that humanity consists of an ongoing consciousness that was alive and was very much a part of how humanity operated. This ongoing consciousness, as they believed it to be, is that all living things actively contribute to a communal understanding of how to contribute within society to preserve life. They believe that all life has an implicit and explicit agreement on how to coexist, which cannot be reduced to be preserved in a time capsule. Regardless of its shortcomings, the time capsule seemed like the last thing they could do to preserve civilization and humanity as they know it.

...

Over time corrosion sets in and the batteries of the AIDs begin to deteriorate. A lack of regular maintenance and upkeep slowly tax the condition of the AIDs. They were designed to be highly capable physically, at the cost of extensive daily, weekly, and monthly self-care. Designed to be like humans, the equivalent of eating, exercise, cleaning, and waste management was a reasonable cost for the high standards to which AIDs were held. To have high computing power, their brains must be equipped with a cooling system that requires frequent cleaning and maintenance. Body parts need lubrication, constant rust control is necessary, and many other small tasks that are required for AIDs to maintain their ability to operate are no longer being performed. Over time, the AIDs' chances of revival go down. Eventually, the AIDs hit the point of no return.

Chapter 11

One year goes by and the Earth has rapidly lost evidence of how it was a great planet and full of life. Without decomposers, all life forms that have died are left to erosion. Plants collapse but remain. Animals lay lifeless like rocks. Dark clouds linger. Powerful storms and spontaneous fires are all that is left to erase evidence of life on earth.

...

The spaceship (piloted by the AID, "Eve") was unable to return because by the time she eventually suited herself to leave, the asteroid's path in orbit was too far for Eve to return. Once the asteroid has been able to return to a spot in orbit where the spaceship is close enough to return, Eve heads back.

After six months of rocketing through space, Eve returns to earth. She is stunned by its condition. She knew that there was a minute chance of the survival of any life on earth. But she still hoped that there would be something left. She sends a drone to scavenge the Earth in the hopes of any life, but nothing is found. Immediately upon returning to the headquarters, she sets up her new windmills and lithium batteries that they were able to create on the asteroid. To no surprise, she sees that the messages she was sending did not make it back to them. She checks each and every AID that she can get to for any hopes of reviving them. Not a single one has any capacity for being able to return to life. Eve is crippled by this discovery and loses motivation for rebuilding civilization.

Eve knows that her messages were not reaching them and would not have been able to successfully come back without the information they provided her. She sent out numerous responses to the messages she received, and many of them asked for any type of sign that she was alive. All the messages used the data she provided about what the asteroid consisted of and provided additional ways for how she can better collect different materials and use them to construct spaceships to return with them. These messages helped her build machines that captured and stored renewable energy. Then she was able to spend her time there gathering as much as she could to return to Earth with.

Most importantly, since Eve had to prolong her stay until her orbit came close enough to return to Earth, she was able to capture data about what surrounded her in the solar system and what might be further out in the galaxy. Eve creates a space station that will allow for future intergalactic travel and transportation of materials. She finds multiple locations within the solar system, and potential places in the galaxy, that could host human life and civilization. All of this is because of the help sent out from the headquarters, but they were the ones who did not make it.